SIGNPOSTS

Unexpected Encounters
of Grace, Mercy & Truth

Dear Austin,
Thank you for
your interest in
my book. Please don't
forget to leave a
review on Amazon
and/or Goodreads.
AC

ALCHRISTIAN VILLARUZ

Published by
Orison Publishers, Inc.
PO Box 188
Grantham, PA 17027
www.OrisonPublishers.com

Acknowledgments

Therese of Lisieux once wrote of God's infinite love and grace: "Your love has been there since before I was born. It has grown as I have grown."

This book is the product of that love in my life, of a love that was present yesterday, is here today, and will be here forever. It is the result of the aspirations and dreams of my Filipino grandparents, who had the audacity to hope for a better life in America because they loved my parents. This volume came about because my mother and father realized that dream, courageously and with great hope, leaving all they knew and loved, and immigrated to America. You are reading my writing because my mother and father's selfless love, guidance and sacrifice set me on the path of learning, and more importantly, on the ways of faith.

I would not have been able to complete this book without the love, support, and understanding of my wife, Diana, and of our sons, Mikhail and Alexander. Our everyday lives served as the inspiration for much of my work; and their patience with my many early mornings and late nights granted me the opportunity to fulfill my lifelong dream of becoming a published author.

You can read this because my old friend, Professor Christopher Shinn, found the time to not only advise and encourage my efforts as a writer but also to edit my writings despite his incredibly busy schedule. And finally, I can share these stories with you because my literary agent, Keith Carroll, saw a potential in my ideas that other agents did not and took a chance on me. So, you see, God's love and grace have been there for me yesterday, today, and forever. And it is to His infinite mercy I dedicate this, my first book.

CONTENTS

Preface .... *ix*

1   Coincidence? *1*

2   Stranger or Admired One? *5*

3   Price of Love *13*

4   Beloved One *31*

5   Broken One *39*

6   Mall Walkers *47*

7   Neighborhood Watch *53*

x   War Machines *59*

8   Communication Breakdown ... *63*

9   Homicidal *73*

10 The Most Important Thing *83*

11 Best Halloween Treat *97*

12 Worse Fates *103*

13 Peace on Earth *107*

Preface

Scripture implores us to show kindness to strangers, for we may well be entertaining angels in disguise. At the same time, our modern lives are meant to be extremely efficient and convenient. With a few omnipotent swipes of our fingers upon our cell phone screens, we can obtain our heart's desire, or seek out answers to what we believe to be life's most profound questions. From a global perspective, we live lives of relative affluence and enviable material ease.

Even minor disruptions to our clean, hassle-free existences—the Wi-Fi going down or perhaps an Amazon delivery arriving later than expected—have come to be construed by many as major inconveniences. We resort to contacting service representatives manning call centers in developing countries who must ponder our First World "problems" with a mixture of incredulity, envy, and disdain.

As an immigrant, military veteran, and emergency physician, I have been placed on a path in my life where I have been compelled to endure many inconveniences which many in our society would much rather avoid. These seeming hassles in my life, which have manifested themselves in always unexpected, sometimes disturbing, but undeniably illuminating encounters with a wide array of human beings included as a sampling that you now find in your possession.

In these pages you will meet with the young and the old, with fellow Christians, but also with Jews and Muslims. You will encounter my neighbors and perhaps come to agree that at times the biggest strangers in our lives are those who live under the same roof as we do. You will meet medical school professors and United States Marines.

You will also encounter the abandoned, the disabled, the ill, and the demented—the flotsam and jetsam of our fast moving, beauty-and-youth-obsessed society—forgotten, smallest and least in our world but still precious to our Creator and with much to teach the rest of us.

I may not have realized it at the time, but in all of these meetings, I am now certain that I was entertaining angels incognito.

In these pages you will travel not only to extreme places like combat zones and emergency departments but also to more mundane locales such as the mall, my neighborhood, and nursing homes.

In these pages you will meet God's people in all of our extraordinary variety. You will meet them as I did—inconveniently, under unintended circumstances, and at times in unpleasant places, but each with their own story and lesson to impart.

These lessons have served as signposts along the road of my life, leading me home throughout my peripatetic existence to dwell in a place our loving Creator intended all along. Indeed, invaluable have been the lessons that these human beings (or undercover angels?) have imparted to me. . .

. . . *Lessons* which I now wish to share with you.

. . . *Lessons* I never would have learned had I chosen not to be inconvenienced so.

. . . *Beauties* I would never have beheld had I chosen to not be hassled.

. . . *Wisdom* I would never have won had I persisted in my relentless pursuit of a clean, convenient, efficient, and very First-World existence.

. . . *Signposts of my life* I would never have taken the time to heed had our Lord not chosen to surprise me by placing these magnificent souls in my path.

The surprises of the Lord have not come to an end! Only He can bring good from misfortune, conjure holiness from a seeming hassle, and turn an inconvenience into an unexpected boon and blessing.

The surprises of the Lord have not come to an end! We entertain angels every day and do not even realize it. I know it is true for me.

May this humble volume remind its readers that it is true for you as well.

❧ I ❧

COINCIDENCE?

I was so tired after a long emergency department shift one night that I almost overlooked a delicate and exquisite miniature tree frog, hanging on for dear life, next to our garage door panel. It must have been blown there by the damaging winds from the severe thunderstorms that had transpired earlier that evening, which I was told, had been violent enough to topple trees.

So fragile and insignificant a creature, clinging yet to life, and delivered to the precarious safety of its current location, beating the odds. Random physics and pure coincidence? Perhaps. Or borne to safety by the breath of God for me to behold and wonder at? Small questions such as these, along with larger questions, like the meaning of suffering in our lives, are questions that we can only answer for ourselves. And the shape our answers take will govern the conduct of our existence.

Coincidence or destiny? Random probabilities or perhaps the will of God at work in our lives? How will we respond when faced with making a choice between believing in fickle fate or seeing events with eyes informed by a fervent faith?

I once saw some patients in the Emergency Room that had been involved in a horrible, head on, roll-over motor vehicle accident on one of our local roads. One of the patients was a young husband, who had been sitting right next to his wife in the rear seat. He escaped relatively unscathed while his wife, who was only a foot or so away from him in the vehicle, was more severely injured and had to be immediately flown from the scene of the accident directly to a trauma center. Unfortunately, the young wife did not survive.

When I learned of this news, I began to ponder the nature of fate and destiny. Do we really have any control over our existence when a triviality as seemingly arbitrary and random as a few feet, or maybe even just a few inches, or what seat you happen to pick when riding in a car is the decisive factor in whether we live or die? Are we truly, solely at the mercy of an uncaring, unfeeling "universe" that doles out our destinies in a chaotic, fickle fashion? Is there absolutely no rhyme or reason to our small, fleeting, and insignificant existences?

Will the only answer to this young man's anguish be "Sorry, but S**t Happens?"

I was informed that the state trooper had already made the death notification to the young husband. I was at the end of my shift, exhausted and fighting off a cold that I had been struggling with for the last few days. All of my instincts at self-preservation were imploring me to not see this unfortunate young husband in addition to the other patients I was finishing up with. *You don't need the drama and heartache right now! Just finish what you've got, then go home and get some rest!* my emergency physician's survival instincts screamed at me.

However, I looked at the tracking board and saw that the emergency room was very busy. If I did not see this young man now, it might be another hour before my relief arrived, and anyone got in to see him. That small, still voice within me, which tells me to take the right and good action, to make the bright, true and honorable choice—a voice which is too often drowned out and overwhelmed by the much louder, pragmatic instincts of self-preservation—this small voice said to me, *Come on now. You know that making these poor people wait anymore is unacceptable. They've already been through enough.*

So, I clicked the "sign up" key on the computer and saw the young husband, perhaps against my own better judgment.

As I discharged him, this young man tearfully asked me, "I don't understand, Doc. She was sitting *right next* to me. Why did *she* have to be *the one* to *die*?"

I instantaneously replied to him, without any fore-thought, and almost automatically, "Maybe the question you should be asking yourself is *Why were you the one who survived*? Maybe there's a plan for you? Maybe there's a destiny for you to fulfill? If you believe in God, maybe He's not done with you yet?"

In other words, it's *not* just that "*S**t happens.*"

I have no idea where this comforting statement came from as I blurted it out. Anyone who knows me knows how abrasive, brusque, blunt, and tactless I can be at times. However, as the young husband squeezed my hand in gratitude and the grieving family in the room looked on in appreciation, I knew I had just said exactly what they needed to hear.

Ultimately, there was a reason that I saw that young husband, and it was to deliver those few, meager words that nevertheless provided some measure of comfort and hope in a time of seemingly overwhelming darkness for him.

In a way, I was *meant to* see him as a patient, I realized.

But I walked out of the room, still not comprehending where those words that I had just said even came from. Certainly it was not from my acerbic, burned out, sarcastic, and often foul emergency physician mouth. However, they had understood. And I cannot explain it.

I left work that night believing I had made a *real difference* for a change.

Perhaps we are not at the mercy of a cold, unfeeling universe. Perhaps events really do happen for a reason. Perhaps our lives are not as arbitrary or random as they sometimes seem to be. Perhaps we do not randomly crash into the other people that enter our lives, like cars in a head-on collision. Perhaps we are placed in the ways of those around us for a purpose.

Perhaps it is not all random.

Perhaps fate and destiny are real. Perhaps, if I listen more to that small, still, oft silenced voice—the voice that tells me to do the right thing, the honorable thing, the good, and beautiful and bright thing—perhaps then I will see that there is a plan and purpose for *all of us.*

Perhaps I had been borne by the breath of God to the young man's bedside, just as the delicate tree frog had been gently and purposefully delivered to the frame of my garage door that stormy night, as reminders that it is not all just mere coincidence. Perhaps that exquisite yet insignificant tree frog and I were precisely where we were intended to be, acting as signposts, pointing to the reality that life is not just a series of random events. Instead, perhaps there is a loving and unique plan for each and every one of us, written in our hearts by One who knew us in the womb.

Perhaps. I am once again tempted towards faith.

❧ 2 ❧

STRANGER OR
ADMIRED ONE?

*Written on the Father's Day when my own fatherhood was
imminent, remembering that perhaps the biggest strangers
in our lives are those of our own household.*

When I was fourteen years old, some relatives of ours
bought some acreage in Lancaster, Pennsylvania. They had
some livestock—cows, chickens, goats, rabbits, and horses—
and invited us to visit. We did so on a beautiful, bright, brisk
and sunny early spring day.

At fourteen, I was caught in the throes of adolescence, as
all fourteen-year-olds are wont to be. I was unsure of myself,
insecure, experiencing the hormonal surges of puberty, all the
while trying to figure out the world and my place within it.

I seemed to be locked in an interminable conflict with my
parents, and with my dad in particular, as I asserted myself and
tested my boundaries, which of course often brought me on a
direct collision course with my father. There were many battles
of the will during my adolescence—it was a time of miscommu-
nications, misunderstandings, and mistakes—when too many
things were left unsaid, or feelings were hurt when far too much
was said, and times when words simply were not enough.

It was a time when it felt like there was an unbridgeable intergenerational chasm between my dad and me. We lived in a state of continuous communication breakdown, it seemed. (I had discovered Led Zeppelin in those days as well.) I resented how much he worked at the time, chasing the American dream, gone nights and weekends, when I thought he should have been at home.

I did not realize it at the time, but now I know that the long hours he put in at work were how he expressed his great love for us. While he had life and strength in his body, never would he allow us to sink into the same soul-crushing poverty that he had experienced during his own youth growing up in post-war Manila.

But, of course, I did not grasp this truth at the time.

I did not understand that, like my pubescent self, my parents also were still trying to figure it all out. Because we recently immigrated to the United States, I should have known that my mom and dad's heads were still spinning from culture shock in trying to reconcile their traditional Asian values of the indissoluble bonds between extended family, duty, obligation, and self-denial, with the frenetic American/Western value system of scattering and dissipation. To my folks, it was an unfamiliar cultural milieu that emphasized freedom, self-fulfillment, self-knowledge, and self-realization—indeed, an endless litany of "selfs" above everything else.

Yes, I should have known better.

But in the folly of youth, I did not.

At the farm in Lancaster was a white stallion, recently purchased by my uncle, grazing in a field. I remember that when my dad saw the stallion, he grinned from ear to ear, which was unusual for him, for in those days he was weighed down by many cares. But not now. He laughed and smiled like a child.

I remember my great surprise when I saw him confidently stride up to the great beast and stroke its mane gently. I saw him put his forehead against the horse's snout and whisper something I could not hear.

He took the horse by the bridle and led it past me into the barn. There my dad proceeded to place a saddle blanket on the horse's back. Upon this covering, my dad placed a heavy western saddle. My dad was not a big man, and I was not anticipating the relative ease with which he heaved the saddle onto the animal's high back. He then proceeded to expertly secure the saddle belt under the great animal's girth, making sure it wasn't too tight by passing a finger between the heavy leather belt and the stallion's abdomen. He proceeded to attach the reins to the bridle and easily adjusted them to the correct length, as if he had done it many thousands of times before.

Imagine the incredulity of my adolescent mind! How did my dad know how to do all of this? He was a white-collar worker, a mild-mannered professional and kind of boring, my unappreciative adolescent psyche assumed at the time. Not really all that exciting of a person. *Where did he learn how to saddle a horse,* I asked myself.

The surprises did not end there.

He secured the reins. Again, my dad was not a big man. Yet with one bound, he mounted the horse without difficulty, naturally, like he had done it many thousands of times before.

At first he spurred the horse on a brisk walk. I saw him lean forward and say something to the animal once again before he spurred the horse onward with his heels. A canter, then a quick trot. From where I stood, I could see my dad's smile and hear his laughter. When he reined the horse in, bringing it to a complete halt, the stallion whinnied in protest. My dad said something to it and stroked its mane. He gave the horse three quick kicks of his heels, giving the stallion his command to go even faster.

What happened next turned my disbelief into complete shock.

My dad took off at a full gallop. . .faster, ever faster. In complete control, my dad had the great beast perform laps at full speed around the field. Then he had the animal swerve abruptly from side to side, followed by rapid switches in direction, barely stopping.

I was afraid for my dad. I thought he might fall.

But all I saw was his bright smile and hear his pure, carefree laughter.

And all I felt was great surprise and absolute wonder about my father. My father? Really? *Who would have thought that Dad could do this,* I asked myself at the time. Is that noble horseman really my dad? Surely not. It could not be! That was my dour, serious, stern, disciplinarian dad?

Surely not. Surely, it was Crazy Horse riding out from the Sioux encampment on the morning of Little Big Horn to defend his people. Surely, it could not be my dad. Instead, was not this figure truly Roland, charging against the Saracens at Roncesvalles, with his great friend Oliver at his side, brandishing his legendary sword, Durandal? It could not be my dad! Surely, this was Theoden on his faithful steed, Snowmane, riding down the Uruk Hai at Helm's Deep when despair fled and hope came with the dawn? Surely, this was not my dad?

But it *was.*

My dad.

For his finale, Dad stopped the mighty stallion in its tracks, pulled back sharply at the reins, and had it rear up on its hind legs. He took off his cap, waved at me, and yelled out, in Filipino accented English, "Hi-Ho Silver!!!!" (It sounded more like "Hi-Hoh Seeelbehhhhr!")

"Holy ****! My dad is the Lone Ranger!" I remember saying to myself, mouth agape, disbelieving completely.

And at that moment, my dad filled me with awe and great joy.

At that moment, my dad WAS Crazy Horse.

He was Roland.

He was Theoden.

He was the Lone Ranger.

He was a *knight*.

But above all, riding that magnificent stallion on that breathtaking spring day, my dad was beautiful. He was joyful. My dad was *holy*, holy at that moment because he was exactly what God had meant him to be.

Afterwards, in the barn, my dad invited me to help him brush the horse down. He reminded me to gently brush the horse's quarters and flanks in a circular motion, while he combed its mane and fed it oats. He gave me a few carrots to feed to the stallion, again reminding me to hold the carrot in my open palm so I did not get accidentally bitten. I remember my dad once again laying his forehead against the horse's snout and saying, *"Ang ganda mo naman."*

(That's Tagalog for "You really are beautiful.")

The horse whinnied its approval and thanks for the compliment. They were made from the same stuff, my dad and that stallion, because on that day, they were both beautiful and holy—exactly as God meant them to be.

I was finally able to overcome my profound incredulity over the extraordinary events that I had just witnessed.

I asked him, "Dad, I didn't know you could ride horses. Where did you learn to ride like that?"

Dad put his arm around me and tussled my hair. It was one of the few moments of truce during our adolescent wars.

Dad smiled and said, "Al, after the war, we had almost nothing. We had lost everything. Our family didn't even have an automobile until I was seventeen years old. How do you think we got around until then?"

I replied, "You guys had to ride horses?"

"That's right! We rode horses and used caratelas. (*Caratela* is Tagalog for horse-drawn carriage.) Your uncles, your aunt, and I all grew up taking care of horses." Dad laughed and tussled my hair again.

And then, I finally understood. In a time rife with misunderstandings, miscommunication, miscues, and mistakes, I experienced a singular moment of sublime epiphany about my father.

And in that moment, I loved and admired him. I was filled with awe and great joy at his exploits, and at contemplating the mythical adventures of his youth in the far-off Philippines. At that moment my dad was the heroic and kind father that all children dream of. He was utterly transformed in my eyes. He became a being of majesty and splendor.

Father's Day is this weekend.

As my own fatherhood becomes more and more imminent, I miss my own father now more than ever. I miss his wisdom, his laughter, his strength, honesty, and toughness. How I yearn for his presence. How I need him! But he was taken from us for reasons known only in the heart of God, I believe.

His loss has created a paradoxical and profound presence of absence within my life, a void, a hurt in my heart made more acute on this weekend during which we honor and remember our fathers.

On this Father's Day, I miss and need my dad now, more than ever.

With modern life and our national culture so rife with snares and traps, all ready and willing to devour our children and lead them astray, we all need our dads more desperately. For we live in a time of false prophets and poseurs, while there exists a great hunger for *real* heroes and authentic heroism. I pray that on this Father's Day, all fathers can be heroic and kind as God meant and created them to be. I pray that all fathers inspire admiration and wonder in their children, as my father did in me on that unforgettable Spring day so many years ago. I pray that all dads become the *real* heroes that their children yearn for and need—kind and not only strong but good and wise as well. I pray on this Father's Day, dads teach their daughters and sons perseverance, toughness, and endurance in hope. That they teach their children how suffering is not random, but that our trials on this earth have meaning. Far too many children have sought escape from their hardships at any cost and are devoured by the aforementioned snares and traps of the world.

Does suffering have meaning? That is perhaps the central question of human existence. And it is our answer to this question that ultimately dictates the conduct of our lives, and whether we are able to make the transition finally from childhood to life as a responsible adult. I pray that all dads teach their children that character is indeed destiny, that adversity and hardship can make us better versions of ourselves. This transformation makes us more ready and willing to help others, exposing the lie of the endless litany of self which threatens always to ruin us.

I pray that on this Father's Day that all dads become holy—exactly what God created them to be. *Ang ganda mo naman!* (You're beautiful!) You are beings of splendor and majesty, the constant and unwavering polestars of our lives, leading us home always during the lonely watches of night, when all other lights have gone out.

And on this Father's Day, I pray that children learn to forgive their fathers, for the times when they fall short for we are all imperfect creatures. Remember, our dads were all probably still trying to figure it all out themselves (as my dad was) while, at the same time, they were doing the very best they could to bring us up. I pray on this Father's Day that we will all be given the grace to cut our dads some slack. I ask God that even though our dads may seem hard, impassive, self-possessed, stoic, and tough that we remember the following words of Norman MacClean:

> *It's true that those who seem the strongest among us are actually the ones that need the most help. . .and in these cases, we have to love completely without completely understanding.*

I pray that on this Father's Day all children can love their dads completely without completely understanding them.

May we forgive our fathers their trespasses!
They are and were not perfect.
But at the very least —they gave us all life.
And where there is life, there is hope.
With this hope in our hearts, all things are possible.

❧ 3 ❧

THE PRICE OF LOVE

The thoughts that go through my mind as I bathe my son.

When my wife, Diana, works late, the task of giving our son, Mikhail, his bath falls to me alone, and I do not mind. So, I put down the lid of the commode and sit on it, turning to the side so I can reach into the tub where my son is sitting so I can wash him. I do it systematically from head to toe.

I wash his dark brown hair, the same color as his mother's. Then I proceed to his face. I scrub and wipe off his eyes and ears, which he inherited from me; then proceed to his nose, which is once again his mother's, realizing that Misha is the perfect synthesis of her and me together.

I behold my son looking up at me, a giggling, wriggling, smiling, striving, reaching, rolling, babbling bundle of humanity, fully alive, that I helped create, who was made in God's own image. The sight of my son fills my heart with such an overwhelming joy that "runneth over" and makes me feel like I will burst out of sheer happiness. It is at this moment I realize that I love Mikhail so completely, so fully, so fiercely and uncompromisingly, with every fiber of my being, that I would give him anything, even my own life. The love and selfless devotion that I feel at these moments tempt my cynical heart

13

into believing something Janice Connell once wrote: "God creates the solution to all the world's problems with each life He weaves together in a mother's womb."

I love my son completely and unconditionally. I have never loved anyone like I have loved him. This realization, as joyful and wonderful as it is, at times conversely fills me with guilt and remorse. Because I realize now that *everyone*, at some point in their lives, has been loved as completely, as fully, and as unconditionally as I love Misha. This realization fills me with shame. Why? Because I would never want my beloved child to be abused or ill-treated by anyone. Yet, I have willfully treated others poorly in the past. I have abused and mistreated others who were someone else's beloved daughter or son.

This realization that I have not necessarily "done unto others" fills me with guilt, regret, and remorse.

It is one of the perils of fatherhood.

When I bathe my son, I am also always haunted by a memory from my time in the military, a time when I saw another father bathing his own beloved son, a time when I bore witness to yet another peril that comes with fatherhood.

It happened back in the summer of 1999 when I was the surgeon in a Marine infantry regiment. Our unit was participating in Operation Allied Force by being thrown into the middle of a genocidal Yugoslavian civil war involving Russian Orthodox Serbs, Muslim Bosnians, and Catholic Croats, in the hopes of ending the killing and bringing some semblance of stability to the region. I remember thinking at the time that this was incredibly naive on their part, given the centuries of feuding, reprisals, lethal tit for tat, and vendettas that had already transpired there.

However, what I found most disconcerting was the fact that just by using external appearances, there was absolutely no way you could tell the difference between a Bosnian, a Croat, or a Serb. They were all Caucasians—light-haired and fair-skinned. Yet they hated each other with an inter-generational, animalistic, primordial hate, deep-seated and intrinsic as if it were written into their DNA. *These people,* I thought, *were, in a way, born to hate.* They knew no other way.

I learned then that sometimes the worst, most potent forms of hatred have nothing to do with skin color.

Far from it, as a matter of fact.

Not long after hitting the ground in the former Yugoslavia, I bore witness to an atrocity that I will never forget. It was a sight that was burned indelibly into my consciousness, an obtrusive memory that is triggered by stressful events at work and returns to trouble me at the most inopportune moments. A therapist I have previously seen used this memory as a basis for diagnosing me with PTSD when I got out of the military.

What I saw was a mass grave. In it were unceremoniously dumped bodies of Bosnian Muslims who had been executed by "Christian" Serbs in a fit of genocidal fervor—male, female, the very young to the very old. Some of the women in the grave were naked. I realized that they had probably been raped before they had been executed.

They were thrown together in an untidy heap as if they were mere garbage with heads here and arms and legs sticking out there. The only characteristic these pieces of human detritus all had in common was a neat 7.62mm bullet hole between their eyes. The stench and the ghastly sight of rats feasting on some of the remains made me vomit. And I was not the only one.

And that is saying something when you are talking about a bunch of hardened Marine infantry.

This and some of the other horrors that cannot be unseen while I was deployed have filled me with a deep cynicism that I quite cannot shake, even though I left the military eighteen years ago. My entire world view has since been jaundiced and tinged by a deep pessimism that I cannot bring myself to overcome, a negativity that aged me prematurely. It really is true—the first casualty of war is innocence.

This mass grave made me think of something Jewish philosopher Kostanty Gebert wrote about Auschwitz: "Auschwitz was a lesson to humanity that man is nothing, man is manure that just happens to be walking in the light."

Man is nothing.

Man is animated manure.

Man is merely meat.

A few days later, our convoy of Humvees and Deuce and a half trucks was halted somewhere outside of Sarajevo. I was sitting on the ground with my back against the rear wheel of our Humvee ambulance, relishing the opportunity to get out of our cramped vehicle and stretch my legs while imbibing MRE coffee. Now and then, small arms fire would erupt in the woods surrounding us, but I paid it no mind. This was my second deployment after all. It seemed that small arms fire was always randomly going off somewhere in our vicinity. Instead of being frightened, I started daydreaming absentmindedly.

I was cruelly shaken out of my reverie by my regimental moniker —"Silver Bullet"—being called out over the radio in our Humvee. I was being summoned to the head of our column, but I didn't know why. I now had to get my gear and

Kevlar on and hustle 150 meters to the head of our column. I muttered expletives all the way.

I arrived to find a group of Marines and a motley looking band of Bosnian militia who had come in under a white flag of truce, surrounding one of my corpsmen. He was on his knees doing CPR on some casualty the Bosnians had carried in on a poncho liner. My corpsman saw that I had arrived and gave a sigh of relief.

However, I saw that as he continued his frantic CPR, there were tears in his eyes. He was a tall, lanky, good-natured kid from northern Wisconsin named Clemmons. He was right out of Corps and Field Medical Service School, and this was his first deployment. The tears, I imagined, were partly because this was the first time this kid from small-town America had ever seen someone who had been shot to death.

I gave the victim a once over as young HN Clemmons continued in his efforts. Clemmons had already cut off the young Bosnian's shirt. I saw that he had been neatly "stitched" by an AK burst with two entrance wounds in the abdomen and chest. This poor kid was probably on the receiving end of some of the small arms fire I had just heard while blissfully sipping my ersatz coffee only minutes before. What did him in, though, was the neat, pencil-sized entrance wound right under his left eye.

I told Clemmons to stop his CPR, and we gently rolled the young man's body over. In the back of his head was a ghastly exit wound—not surprising as the Serbs were using steel jacketed AK rounds—that had blown out the occipital lobe of his brain and his cerebellum, perfectly exposing his posterior cranial fossa. With my physician's clinical detachment, all I could think at the time was how it reminded me of some Frank Netter anatomy sketch that I had seen as a medical student. The wound that had left the young Bosnian's face almost untouched was belied by the gory mess that the back of his head had become. Just looking at this kid's face, you would have thought that he was just sleeping.

But in reality, this kid was toast.

Burnt toast, to be clear.

I gently put my hand on Clemmon's shoulder and told him to stop his CPR. Tears were still streaming down his face. He would not stop. I grasped his shoulder more firmly and said, "Clemmons, you did what you could here. This kid was dead before you even got to him. Nothing you could do. It's over."

Clemmons finally stopped but continued to sob. I had one of the Marines call one of my more senior corpsman to our location so he could see to young Clemmons and hopefully calm him down a bit.

I looked at the Marines and the Bosnians. I drew the fingers of my right hand repeatedly over my neck in the cold, pragmatic, universal gesture of a life just snuffed out. His comrades looked down in disbelief and sadness. Clearly, they had liked the newly deceased young man. Like Clemmons, some of them started to weep. They knelt beside the body to say their goodbyes.

They asked through an interpreter if we could see to the dead man's remains. They were "on the move," they explained, and not able to tend to the corpse. By "on the move" what I believed they really meant was that they were going to inflict some payback on whatever Serbs they could find in recompense for their comrade's killing.

Tit for tat, for time immemorial.

Our convoy commander gave his approval for us to take

possession of the young Bosnian's remains. The Marines produced a US government issue body bag, and we placed the dead Bosnian in it. I led a procession of Marines and corpsmen that carried the body to a Deuce and half truck a few vehicles back from the ambulance in which I was riding.

The corpse was heaved, rather crudely, into the back of the truck, as the Marines and sailors were only too eager to divest themselves of such a hefty burden on what was a very hot day. The body bag landed with a thud onto a pile of MRE boxes and bottled water, just like it was another piece of freight or luggage.

So futile. . .what the hell are we doing here? I thought to myself.

After all, man really is just manure.

Truthfully, unlike young Clemmons, as a physician going on my third year with Marine Grunts, I was completely unmoved by the entire spectacle. I was hard. As I related earlier, I had become cynical and jaded, I had lost almost all of my empathy and innocence. I brusquely brushed the entire episode off. Then, still intent on taking advantage of the halt in our movements, I set my sleeping mat onto the ground beside my vehicle, and using my ALICE pack as a pillow, I covered myself with my flak jacket as a precaution and proceeded to take a much-needed nap.

I couldn't have been asleep for more than a few minutes when Clemmons shook me awake.

"Clemmons. . .what the ****?!" I said groggily.

He replied, "Dr. Villaruz, sir, Colonel Moore has a situation he wants you to deal with."

Colonel Moore was our XO, and well, when the XO talked, I listened. But I was still angered at being awoken prematurely, muttering yet more expletives under my breath as I put my body armor and Kevlar back on.

Clemmons led me to the tree line where a group of Grunts from our security detail was warily pointing their weapons at an elderly Bosnian couple leading a decrepit looking donkey pulling an even more decrepit looking donkey cart. The old woman wore the traditional head scarf of a Muslim woman that has come of age.

The old couple were trembling and scared witless, but I could also sense a quiet determination, an unspoken resolve in them that was willing to brave any danger to achieve some task they obviously deemed to be absolutely necessary. They possessed a natural, wordless kind of dignity that demanded respect in return, so that even the grizzled Marine Corporal who subjected them to the indignity of a body search did so with a level of gentleness and deference that was rarely seen in our little infantry world.

Our interpreter arrived and spoke to them. The old man produced a picture and handed it to me. It was a photo of a smiling young man, wearing a suit, who was standing with crossed arms in front of a rose bush in full bloom. What struck me the most about the photo is that it could have been the graduation photo of any high school kid in America as well—your son, nephew, or maybe the kid down the street. He looked like a happy, nice person, the kind of kid any parent would be proud to call their child. And I recognized the face instantly. It was the young man in the body bag that we had just dumped in back of the truck like so much baggage, like a piece of mere meat.

The interpreter explained what was already obvious to me. These were his parents. They were here to claim his body. The interpreter went on to explain that in Islamic culture, it is absolutely imperative that the dead be buried as soon as possible.

The parents were here to perform one final act of love for their dead son.

I cleared it with Colonel Moore on the radio, who approved the transfer of the remains to the parents. I then radioed the Gunny in charge of the logistics section to get a working party together in order to deliver the body bag to the family. This was completed with the usual Marine Corps efficiency.

The body bag was laid at the parent's feet. They knelt down beside it. The old man's arthritic hands fumbled with the zipper, so I helped him open the bag with more than a little trepidation. I was not looking forward to their reaction once they saw what kind of condition their son's head was in. I slowly pulled aside the top of the flap, revealing their son's deceptively intact face.

Far from the dramatics and emotional diarrhea I was expecting, their grief was instead expressed in a dignified and understated kind of way. They stroked their dead child's face, and both began to weep quietly. The old man looked up towards heaven and holding his hands up in the Orans position of prayer, he muttered a supplication, the only words of which I could understand being "Insh-Allah, Insh-Allah" ("God willing, God willing").

Sorry, old man, but I think God left Yugoslavia a long time ago, I thought to myself cynically.

But remembering my own parents, I was in reality deeply moved by the entire sad, pathetic spectacle, for even then I realized that having to bury your own child is one of the perils of fatherhood. One of the perils of parenthood.

The father said something that the interpreter translated for me. He said, "The father wants to wash the body before they take it. It is their tradition to wash the body before burial. They need your help, Doctor."

I was about to protest, and tell them not just no, but that I would not permit them to wash the body while our convoy was just sitting out here, exposed and in the open, with no cover whatsoever, drawing fire—a soft target if there ever was one. But something in the way the mother gently stroked her dead child's face and brushed his hair—her every gesture saying that no matter what, come what may, he would always be her baby, made me relent. I said resignedly, "Well. . .so, what kind of help do they need?"

Through the translator, I learned that some Croats or Serbs had poisoned their village water supply by throwing some dead animals into it. They had no clean water to wash their son's body.

"Okay," I replied. I radioed the logistics gunny again and before long, some Marines appeared with several five-gallon Gerry cans of non-potable water, along with some tarps. Clemmons and some Marines then moved the body bag to an area further away from our vehicles in case they ended up drawing fire from any nearby Serbs. I thought our involvement in the entire sorrowful spectacle was concluded at that juncture.

However, Clemmons came up to me and said, "Sir, if it's okay with you, I'd like to help the family wash their son's body."

I was about to tell him no, he was being a pain in the rear, and I did not want him exposed in the open like that; it was too risky. If the parents wanted to risk themselves, that was their business, but I would not allow Clemmons to do so. However, there was such a small-town American wholesome earnestness to Clemmons' request that I almost relented. Then, the thought of having to write a letter to Clemmons' parents telling them that their son had been KIA because I had authorized this stunt hardened my heart again.

I was about to deny his request, but an African American Marine Sergeant named Burke, who was watching this pathetic episode unfold, unexpectedly said to me, "Sir, we'll provide security if Clemmons wants to help," and motioned to his squad of Marines, who had been the first to see the elderly Bosnian couple emerging from the tree line. I saw the Sergeant's Marines were nodding in agreement with him. This show of magnanimity and mercy from the Grunt Marines took me by surprise. Their usual attitude towards the plight of yet more down on their luck civilians caught in the crossfire was at worst outrightly dismissive, and at best, completely indifferent.

None of us had wanted to get this involved, this entangled. Yet here was an unexpected kindness in a place filled with so much casual cruelty.

For apparently, Clemmons and I were not the only ones moved by the sad situation in which these parents found themselves.

I relented.

I nodded to Sergeant Burke. He gave a few curt orders to his Marines. They calmly locked and loaded, then fanned out and disappeared silently into the tree line with grim and practiced determination, using only hand signals to communicate. They moved with a purpose. They did not hesitate. They meant business and prepared a nasty surprise for those wishing to disrupt the funerary proceedings. I was happy and proud to have such men on our side.

Security? Check. So, I turned to Clemmons and said, "Showtime, Clemmons. Get it done."

Clemmons helped the parents roll their child's body out of the body bag and onto the tarps. They then stripped the body of all clothing. Clemmons then poured water from the heavy five-gallon cans while the parents, on their knees, washed their child's body from head to toe.

At first his mother was helping, but she stopped early on. She just could not bring herself to do it. I was grateful for that. I did not want her to see what a grotesque mess the back of her child's head had become—the head she supported in the bend of her arm when he was a newborn. Yes. Thankfully, Mom stopped early on. She remained kneeling, arms at her sides, fists clenched in anguish, head thrown back, sobbing silently, eyes shut tightly against the horror she could no longer bear. She could not go on.

It was all up to the father now. With Clemmons' assistance, he alone would perform this one final act of devotion for his lost son, one final dignity for his beloved child in the face of centuries of reckless hate, inhumanity, and misery, which had now devoured his son as well.

Looking back across the intervening decades, I still remember this father bathing his lost son. I remember him whenever I bathe my own son, for the manner of washing was very similar.

Just as I wash Misha, I remember the old man washing his own son's hair, the same color as his. Next, he scrubbed his dead son's eyes and ears, which he appeared to have inherited from his mother, and then to his nose, which was once again his father's. He washed this dead child that was the perfect synthesis of him and his sobbing wife. There were no happy giggles or shrieks of protest at this bathing, though. There were no bath toys to offer distraction—only a somber silence.

The father proceeded, systematically, as I wash my own son, careful to get the little spaces between the fingers and toes. The father proceeded. He did not cry. His expression was one of grim determination, every bit as convincing as the one worn by the Marine Infantrymen starting to gather and watch the ritual. The old man did not utter a peep. He had a mission. But in his eyes, I could see the anguish and torrents of emotion within him. In his eyes I could see his strength. I could see his defiance.

In performing this one final act of devotion for his precious child, this withered old man was obstinately telling this cynical, fallen, flawed, and jaded world:

"My son is not manure!"

"My son is not merely meat!"

"He is my beloved son!"

This father's single-minded determination, his sheer effort of will, his defiance, his conviction, his courage had clearly won the admiration and respect of the Marines who had come to witness. There were no wiseacre remarks, no profanities from the Marines. Just a respectful silence. And we are talking about Marine Grunts here.

One of the Marines who had come to watch was the head of the Regimental Comms section. His name was Master Sergeant Ritchie. Top Ritchie hailed from Georgia and was a devout Southern Baptist. I remember that he would quote from the Bible at seemingly random moments, like some righteous Old Testament prophet. Despite his eccentricities, he was a celebrity within the regiment because Top was a survivor of the 1983 Islamic terror bombing of the Marine barracks in Beirut.

I remember doing his re-enlistment physical and seeing X-rays of his shattered right hip and of the shrapnel that was still in his right leg— injuries he had sustained in the bombing. Top Ritchie walked with a slight limp but somehow always mustered up the grit to pass the PRT twice a year. As Marines go, Top was introspective, quiet, reticent, and kind of cranky even, often bordering on insubordination—all no doubt the result of his previous harrowing experiences. But the younger Marines adored him, and officers, mindful of the Purple Heart Top wore on his dress blues, gave him plenty of leeway.

Top Ritchie nodded at me. I nodded back.

He watched as the old man washed his dead child's corpse. Top seemed to be contemplating, remembering.

He then did something I did not expect. He unstrapped his Kevlar helmet and took it off, out of respect for the old couple's loss. He bent his head forward and closed his eyes.

I realized that Top was praying silently.

Now if there if there was anyone in the Regiment who had cause to despise and hate Islam in all of its forms, it was Master Sargent Ritchie. But no. I guess at heart he would always remain a Southern gentleman and a true Christian who believed that Jesus loves *all* of us, yes He does—and He will make all things new one day.

So, following Top's cue, all of us—enlisted, officers, boots, salty vets, pogues, Grunts, Corpsmen, Marines, and sailors— all of us silently took off our Kevlars out of respect for the dignity, the courage, the love and the devotion that we were now witnessing.

The father, though, was oblivious to all of this. He would not be distracted from the task at hand.

The father was making progress. Because of his efforts and the cleansing, purifying waters dispensed by Clemmons, his son's body was being transformed from being a bloody grotesque mess into a sight that could be beheld without inducing complete revulsion. Then the time came to roll the body over, exposing the gory exit wound at the back of the young man's head. I thought that this sight would certainly give the old man pause, but it did not.

The same hands that supported his son during his first faltering steps as an infant proceeded with the same stoic determination. The old man gently washed the bits of bone and brain from the light brown hair that framed the hideous wound, careful to not cut his fingers on the jagged bits of shattered cranium. As the old man probed what remained of his child's head, I thought of what Doubting Thomas said in the Gospel, "Not unless I place my hands in his wounds will I believe."

Could you imagine the unspeakable horror of beholding your own offspring's brains? My God. But the old man continued, nonetheless. He continued defiantly, obstinately. Courageously.

"My son is not meat! My son is not manure! My beloved son has dignity, and I will show you!" his tortured visage cried out. "My son will be buried properly! No faceless anonymity of a mass grave for him!" His maddened eyes screamed, "You Marines think you know what courage is? I'll show you real courage!"

He proceeded in his grim task with a love for his child that was big enough to swallow the horror and despair that threatened to overwhelm him, proving that the opposite of fear is not courage. The opposite of fear is love. For only love could sustain him as he fulfilled his grisly and unspeakable task.

As I slather Mikhail in moisturizer after his bath, I am reminded of what the old man did after he finished washing his son's corpse. He anointed his child's broken body not with

a curative cream—for his wounds were beyond any healing—
but with some kind of balm that smelled pleasantly and sooth-
ingly of cedar and wildflowers, contrasting sharply with the
acrid aroma of cordite that resulted from the firefights going
on around us. The balm was poured from a heart-shaped vial
that his wife produced by reaching into her robes, into her
bosom. The fact that she had hidden the vial there was indic-
ative of the balm's great value.

After his moisturizer, I dress Misha in cheerful pajamas as
he prepares for bed, pajamas emblazoned with endless stars,
soft clouds, smiling teddy bears, somnolent sheep, and friendly
puppies—all the aphorisms of a fleeting, gentle, and sheltered
childhood. But for this couple's dead son, there was only a
plain, unadorned, dazzlingly white and immaculate shroud
with which they covered their dead child's remains. *Attire very*
appropriate to meet our Maker in, I thought, *on that great and*
terrible day when all will be revealed.

And with that final gesture, the father and Clemmons
were done.

Spontaneously, out of respect, Clemmons, Top Ritchie
with his shattered hip, myself, and a few Marines then loaded
the corpse into the decrepit donkey wagon pulled by an even
more decrepit looking donkey. The dead man's humanity had
been restored by his father's love, and we did not heave him
into the cart like a piece of freight or luggage, as he had been
previously heaved into the truck. No, we laid him into the cart
gently, like he was a friend. A brother.

For he, his father had reminded us, was not merely meat.

The parents gathered their belongings to go. The old
woman continued to weep silently. The old man, not making eye contact but now no longer trembling in fear, nodded

once to no one in particular. It was a solemn, understated but very dignified gesture of leave-taking. . .a defiant good-bye that reminded us that while a real man may be completely destroyed, he can never be completely defeated.

The father was giving us one final obstinate reminder in the face of all the death, despair, and suffering that comes with genocide, "My son is not manure! My son is not mere meat!"

Then the old woman and the old man, their task complete, took their dead child and departed on what would be their last journey together in this world, disappearing into the tree line.

"*Inshallah, Inshallah.*" I thought to myself as they departed. *God wills it.*

We never saw them again.

But I will never forget them.

In fact, I think of that father bathing his child every time I bathe my own son. It is an unbidden memory, an unpleasant one. It is a dark specter that never fails to over-shadow what should be a happy time with my Misha. I wish I could un-remember it. I wish I could unsee it. But I cannot. It is an unbidden, unpleasant, and very undesirable figment of my past, a hidden price incurred by my service to this country.

As much as this memory torments me, it is very instructive as well.

Fatherhood has been the most joyful adventure in my life, along with marriage, but the experience of watching the Bosnian parents remains a potent reminder that fatherhood is a double-edged sword.

Fatherhood is perilous.

There is the unspeakable possibility that your child might be taken from you. You might have to bear the unbearable, endure what cannot be endured, as that Bosnian father did so many years ago.

Fatherhood is dangerous.

Fatherhood can mean having to say goodbye, and one day incur a cost, a price that it may break my heart to pay. Fatherhood makes you vulnerable. You live in fear of having to make an unspeakable sacrifice of something you value more than anything, more than your own life.

Love has a price.

The defiant look in that old Bosnian man's eyes saying: "You Marines think you know what courage is?!" made me realize that it is not war that makes a man.

Love does.

For courage does not dispel fear.

Love does.

A father's love.

As I bathe my own laughing and joyful son, I recall Clemmons' cleansing, purifying waters poured out over the body of a dead man in one final act of mercy. The sublime and the horrific simultaneously occupy my consciousness, and I realize that love can involve loss. Love can cost. Love has a price.

Loss and pain are the price we pay for loving—the horrific and the sublime.

It is one of the perils of fatherhood.

And I am haunted by memories of purifying waters and recollections of the final acts of love.

❧4❧

BELOVED ONE

Written during my singlehood. A reminder that the end is not really the end—it is the beginning.

"Are you married?" she asked me in a moment of lucidity.

"Oh no," I replied, but added hopefully, "I'm still looking, though."

"So, what are you looking for?" she questioned me further.

I thought about it. Then I said, "I think the most important quality is kindness. The second most important trait is intelligence. Then, it would be nice if she were pretty too."

This was hardly original on my part. I ripped it off from Van Morrison's song, "Sweet Thing," where he sings of a woman with "a saint-like smile, a beautiful mind, and the champagne eyes." Hardly original on my part, yes, but for me it does ring true.

She digested that for some moments, then replied, "I would have married you."

I blushed. My discomfort caused amusement among those sitting around us.

She continued proudly, "I was all those things when I was young. But I'm sorry to disappoint you—I met my husband first!" she said with a wry grin. There were more laughs from those around us. Then she added somberly, "He was the love of my life. But he's gone now." Her eyes, until now filled with humor, fell when she said this.

Normally, this would be an exchange I would have been flattered to have with any woman. However, the woman in this case was a demented, octogenarian resident of the nursing home where I volunteer. It is a residence for homeless elderly. Compounding this woman's destitution was her profound loneliness. She was unvisited in the nursing home—her remaining relatives have essentially abandoned her. It is a pitiable existence. The occasion of our conversation was lunch, as I was helping to feed her, spooning food into her mouth. A massive stroke had left her wheelchair bound and unable to care for herself.

Thinking of her lost husband saddened the old woman. She said, "I've lost my appetite. Please excuse me. Can you please take me back to my room? There's something I'd like to show you."

"Yes, ma'am, of course," I replied. I took off her bib, cleaned her face off, and wheeled her back to her room.

On the nightstand by her bed was a sepia-toned black-and-white picture. The rest of the room was essentially bare and very spartan in nature. As far as I could tell, this picture was her only possession.

"I wanted you to see this picture," she said.

The photo, edges cracked with age, was of her and her husband, World War II era, judging from the Army sergeant's uniform he was wearing. Being a former military man, I took note of his decorations—Bronze Star, Purple Heart, European Campaign Medal—the Greatest Generation made manifest in manhood. I looked at this image of the woman's younger self, beaming at the camera. She had indeed been very beautiful as she had told me.

However, what really struck me was her husband's gaze. For in the photo, he was not gazing into the camera lens. Her long dead husband was gazing at her in the photo, and his look was one of deep affection and love but also one of great admiration, esteem—even awe—for her. It was clear from the look on his face that he treasured her immensely and not just for the fleeting moment captured by the camera—but forever. Because real love never dies.

In the ancient photo, her husband's gaze seemed to say, "This is my kind-hearted one, my beautifully minded one, my 'face that launched a thousand ships' one. This is my beloved." She had been his "sweet thing." His gaze said, "Here at last is my heart's desire. I have finally found the moon amidst all the dying stars of night."

Clearly, the old woman had been beloved.

She asked me to hand her the photo. I did. She looked at it lovingly and said, "This was my husband. He fought in the war, and I *waited* for him. This picture of us is from when he got home. We were so happy then. There was so much hope in those days."

"I dream of him always," she said, looking at the photo of him with tenderness and joy.

She then closed her eyes and clasped the old photo to her chest. The old woman then said to me, "Thank you for everything today, dear. I'd like to be left alone now."

I clutched her shoulder affectionately and made my exit, leaving her to feast on her sacred memories. *Let her eat her fill and drink to her heart's content,* I thought. For in our memories, as well as in our hearts, we are always young, clear-eyed, beautiful, and vigorous. *Let her feast! It may be the only joy she has left. Let no one take that last thing from her.*

I continue to see this beloved woman on my volunteer days. She has good days and bad days, as old, demented people do. Some days she remembers who I am; sometimes she does not. However, knowing she had been beloved changed the way I thought of her and her pathetic circumstances in a way that *I will always remember.* For I realized it had not always been so for her, as it has not always been so for so many in our fallen and flawed world.

I saw her now not as a pitiful, forgotten, ailing, homeless, and completely dependent old woman. She seemed to me as a once noble queen who had now fallen on hard times. She had been a beloved one but now exiled by death from her king, and she continued to pine for him even now, as faithful as Penelope, just as she waited for him to return from the battlefields of Europe all those years ago. Yes, she was once a beloved, awe-inspiring, and captivating queen, now fallen on hard times, her rightful majesty and splendor obscured.

However, it was not always so.

Nor will it *always be* so.

As a physician, I know that this woman is not long for this earth. Her age and multiple co-morbidities assure this. I know one day soon I will arrive at the nursing home, seek her out to take her to her meal, and find her room empty, cleaned out, and waiting for a new occupant. She would be gone.

Gone. All her memories of a woe-be-gone world, her wisdom, valuable insights, perceptions, knowledge, advice, hopes, dreams, and heart's desires, *all gone*, never to be repeated again, as these qualities were uniquely present in this one beloved as they are uniquely present in *all of us.* For it is true, when some one dies, a whole world—their interior hidden world, known only to them—dies along with them.

Working with the elderly has made me acutely aware of this. When one of my elderly friends passes on, a whole inner world dies, never to be repeated because it is unique in its expression within each individual person. An inner world perishes—one just as real as, perhaps more real than, the one we can behold with our mere senses.

I will probably not be there when my friend, this beloved one, the hidden queen, passes on. But I like to think, I like to *hope*, it will be while she dreams.

In her lonely and troubled sleep, she will hear a voice that will call her out of her misery and speak to the deepest desires of her heart. The voice will lead her back to that place where there is so much hope for her—an enduring hope which never fails. She will be surprised at the quickness and readiness of her response in this place of hope. Indeed, she will respond as if she were young again.

Am I young again? she will ask herself in her sleep. *In heaven, aren't we supposed to be the age that we were when were most joyful in life?* she will wonder.

The voice will say, "Rise up, awaken, my beautiful one, my dove! Come then my love, my lovely one, come. For see, winter is past, the rains are over and done. Let me see your face! Let me hear your voice! For your voice is sweet, and your glance is inviting."

Eyes still closed, she will tell herself, *For some reason this dream seems a lot more real than my other ones.*

The voice will continue, "Arise, my fair one, for your journey over the mountains of sacrifice, your exile, has come to an end. The flowers are in bloom and the call of turtledoves is once again heard in the land. No longer are you forsaken. No longer will you be called desolate. For my heart finds its delight in you. I have found you again, and you will now be called beloved once more."

Eyes still closed, she realizes that the voice, though she has not heard it in a long time, sounds like the one that is most precious to her. Her heart leaps with joy—a heartfelt happiness that she has not felt in many years.

The voice will continue, "Don't you see, my beautiful one, my love? I know your suffering has been great. I have missed you so much! But don't you remember? For something new to begin, something old has to end first. It must always be so! Something old must always end in order for something new to begin."

She realizes that she knows that voice for sure. It is the voice of him whom her heart loves. She still thinks she is dreaming. Then she finally decides to open her eyes and realizes that she is not dreaming at all.

Her sergeant is standing there, looking at her with great love, joy, desire, and *awe*. Her husband has the same admiring expression on his face that he did in the photograph taken so many years ago. He beckons her, saying, "But now is not the time for endings, my beloved. This is the beginning."

Her youth restored, splendid again as the rainbow gleaming against brilliant clouds and as stunning as wildflowers in the days of spring, she arises once again to meet the one whom her heart has always loved.

And so, the beloved is beloved once again, here at the beginning of things, beloved, now and forever. Her exile is finally over.

May it be so for her.

Yes, may it be so for my friend, the hidden queen. The beloved. She is hidden but never forsaken. Beloved and never forgotten.

For this is not an ending.

It is a beginning.

❧ 5 ❧

BROKEN ONE

Who indeed are the broken ones?

Sometimes in the midst of our hectic and often heedless lives, the veil between worlds is lifted. We get a glimpse of heaven, and this epiphany quite literally stops us in our tracks. And yes, sometimes we need to be *stopped*.

I walked into the ER to work a night shift recently. It was a mess—waiting room full, patients in the back already waiting hours to be seen, family members standing outside of rooms, arms akimbo, standing impatiently, staring down any staff that happened to walk by, letting their displeasure regarding the wait time be known.

As I walked in, being a Tolkien aficionado, I thought to myself: *Lord, just once—once—I'd like to walk into this place at night and not feel like Theoden felt when he and the Rohirrim arrived at Minas Tirith to behold the entire host of Mordor arrayed on the Pelennor Fields before the besieged White City. Just once.*

So, of course, I went into crisis mode and proceeded to do that thing that I do very well. I went into "Belt Fed Pit ER Doctor Mode." (Belt Fed as opposed to semi-automatic or even burst; ER Doc Mode is a mental zone many of us enter when confronted with daunting clinical situations such as this when the ER is quite literally overwhelmed.)

I push a 27-year-old pace out of my 47-year-old body, beginning to work through patients. It is probably not very good for my health. In this mode, it pays to be clinically detached, objective, and pragmatic because this allows for the rapid decision making required. Emotions, you have been taught, only cloud the essential issues. You only retain the bare minimum of empathy required so you do not seem completely cold and robotic to your patients.

You go from room to room, coldly weighing risk/benefit ratios, breaking bad news, and lowering expectations with emotional distance, street smarts, and above all, with a firmness implying you will brook no argument. Because things *need to happen. Now.* It is no surprise that the emblem of the American Board of Emergency Medicine is an hourglass because in our little ER world, *time* is always of the essence.

The dispensing of Emergency Medicine in a belt fed manner is all very efficient, and of course, productive. My ammo was inexhaustible. I was in my zone.

The pitfall to all of this mindset, of course, is that you can become reckless with the feelings of others. You can forget how what you do and say affects your patients and your co-workers. You have come to see people not as people, at times, but merely as another set of problems that you must solve with not much time. Patients cease to have names and become mere diagnoses with which you must contend.

You sometimes come to see them, tragically, as a burden, even. You forget that there is a living, breathing, and feeling person at the receiving end of your actions, words, and decisions. You can forget this reality because you have become that

Belt Fed ER Doc that four years of residency, a military background which valued "the mission" above all else, and sixteen years of experience have transformed you into.

You realize, in your quiet hours, that at times you are really more of a technician, tradesman—or like an automaton or machine perhaps—than a physician who should value human relationships with patients more than anything else.

You realize you may have become a 47-year-old that your 27-year-old self may not have been proud of.

So, there I was in Belt Fed Pit ER Doc Mode.

My next patient was a young child with cerebral palsy. She had a severe form of the disease and was non-verbal. The patient was in the room with her mother.

I proceeded to obtain the history from the mother with the aforementioned clinical detachment, still cool, calculating, managing my time and slightly rushed, as usual. I noted Mom's clothing: shabby, obviously not affluent or very stylish, but clean and pressed. And I noticed that the little girl, despite her contracted frame and profound debility, which I am sure made dressing her very difficult, was well dressed in a sweater and jeans. This little girl was truly cared for, I saw.

She was *loved.*

Mother and daughter's appearance and demeanor told me: "Yes, we are poor. We don't have much. But we have our dignity."

I inquired after the father. Long gone. "She's all I have in the world," Mom said, looking at her child lovingly.

True, they don't have much, I thought, *but they certainly have each other.*

Then I proceeded to examine the tiny, deformed, fragile, and silent little girl. As I sat the little girl up to listen to her lungs, she did something surprising.

She grabbed my hand, smiled at me, then kissed my palm lightly. I was surprised, sure, for unexpected displays of affection take me aback, but I did not withdraw my hand. How could I? She was so small, pathetic, insignificant, vulnerable, hidden, pitiable, and overlooked by the world around her. How could I withdraw my hand? To do so would be cruel and inhumane—an abomination in the annals of personal interaction.

The little girl then proceeded to inspect my right arm, not letting go of it. She looked at the scar on my forearm where I had an incision and drainage of a methicillin resistant Staphylococcus Aureus abscess that I had doubtless contracted from a patient. She touched the scar lightly and looked at me inquisitively, and in her non-verbal manner asked me, "How did you get that scar?" She then mouthed the word "OUCH" as she looked at the scar. It is an unattractive scar that I am self-conscious about, but I was not embarrassed when this little girl investigated it. I was not taken aback.

Instead, I was deeply moved.

I helped her mother lay her daughter's tiny, wizened body back onto the bed so I could complete the exam. The girl grabbed my right hand again and placed her head in it. She then proceeded to caress her own face gently using my hand, signifying that I should do the same, turning her head to look at me as she did so. Again, I was strangely not taken aback by this display of physical affection. She looked me right in the eye.

Despite her many ailments, the little girl's eyes were bright and clear, perceptive and questioning. Her eyes were dancing, happy and sad at the same time, and hopeful too. They projected an inner peace and joy I cannot explain. Through them, you could tell there was an intelligence present in her tortured body. Despite her silence, she was capable of deep feeling and possessed of a vibrant inner emotional life. I could see that despite her insignificance and smallness in the eyes of the world, she possessed a depth of character, emotion, and thought that dwarfed that possessed by many of her supposedly more fortunate fellow humans.

She looked me right in the eye, and I could not avert my gaze. She continued to stroke her own face using my hand.

Her eyes questioned me wordlessly, "Do you see me, Dr. Villaruz? I mean *really see me?* You're always so busy being competent, efficient, and productive. Yes, you are good at what you do. But do you *really see us?* Will you be cold, calculating, detached, and pragmatic with *me* too? Because I see *you*, Dr. Villaruz. I see your scars, and I'm not even afraid to touch them."

"I *see you*. But do *you* see me? Do you see *us?* I mean *really* see *us?*"

As we looked at each other and this unspoken dialogue transpired between us, I began to understand what John Paul II wrote about regarding the terminally ill: "For anyone who appears completely at the mercy of others and is radically dependent upon them, can only communicate through the silent language of the profound sharing of affection."

Do you really see me?

I fell out of Belt Fed ER Doc Mode with no desire to return. Time and efficiency, always so paramount, ceased to become an issue during this wordless "profound sharing of affection" with this small, but unexpectedly mighty, complete stranger. Indeed, time ceased to exist. I had been stilled, no check that, *stopped* in my tracks by this tiny, seemingly powerless human being.

I noticed that I was now stroking her little face of my own volition; as she rested her head on my hand, her eyes closed.

Cradling her tiny head felt like a little swallow had alighted onto my hand, and if I squeezed too hard, I might hurt it. She had ceased to become a patient, a mere diagnosis for me to contend with. This little one was now my own little sister, and I realized meeting her was no coincidence for she had been put in my path for a reason.

Because I needed to be *stopped*.

I had been cold, detached, unfeeling, almost completely devoid of any empathy, and worst of all, reckless with the feelings of others. I needed to be stopped.

In that moment, I became filled with remorse, regret, and guilt. I realized that it was not this pathetic, small, chronically ill little one that was the broken one.

I was the one that was truly broken.

Broken. Blinded by pride and ego. Too competitive. Arrogant. Obsessed with efficiency and productivity at the expense of human relationships. Impatient. Selfish. Cynical. Always assuming the worst. Sometimes, overly confident in my knowledge and skills. Sarcastic. Not listening. Stubborn. Detached. Lacking in empathy. Heedless. Reckless. Broken.

Broken, despite all my worldly successes.

I was the broken one. And I came to the realization that these small ones, these silently suffering ones, these hidden ones, these forgotten ones, these weak ones, these helpless ones, these disfigured ones, these completely dependent ones—these were more precious to God and closer to Him than I was and more beautiful to Him too. For they are possessed of that unvarnished, unsullied, and terrifically clear inner light that never goes out.

Do we see *them*?

And the realization of this, as I stood there, stilled and stopped in my tracks, silently caressing this little one's face, made me tear up. However, "not all tears are evil," as Tolkien also wrote. Her mother noticed, came up to me, and put her arm around me.

"It's okay, doctor," she said. "It's okay. I know it's hard, but we're all going to be okay. We have to believe that. We have to have faith." This woman, though I heedlessly thought her shabby just minutes before was in truth the wealthiest person in the world.

The three of us, complete strangers—a sick child, an overwhelmed single mom, and a jaded ER doctor—arms entwined, shared a few moments of incredible peace and comfortable silence together in the midst of all the ER chaos, with its alarms sounding and bustle, only the opening of a curtain away. In that sublime moment, the veil between worlds parted, and I glimpsed heaven.

I reflected about this incident later as I was driving back home after the end of my shift. I prayed about it. And I heard an inner voice, not audible, yet as strong and as clear the sound of trumpets on the battlements of Minas Tirith calling me home, which said, "You are strong, Al. Sometimes too strong. You needed to be broken. You needed to be humbled. You needed to be *stopped*."

Thank You, Lord, for this gift of being humbled and broken. Thank You, Lord, for *stopping* me. Because it is when I forget that You—and not my own efforts—are the source of everything good in my life, that I lose my way and get into trouble. Thank You for reminding me in this tiny, fragile but truly majestic person, what was written in the Old Testament, The Lord does not look at the things people look at. "For God sees not as man sees, for man looks at the outward appearance, but the Lord looks at the heart" (1 Sam. 16:7).

And thank You, Lord, for giving me such a gentle, loving, and above all unexpected little messenger to remind me of this profound truth. The surprises of the Lord have not come to an end! Thank You for being merciful because I know that the lesson could have been much harsher and left a much bigger scar than the one on my forearm.

Do we see them? I mean *really see* them?

These destitute ones, these dejected ones, these down-trodden ones, these derelict ones, these denigrated ones—do we really see them? I mean *really* see them? They do not need our competence, our efficiency, our knowledge, our money, or our decisiveness. They do need our time, our caring, our understanding, our compassion, and our empathy. They need our touch.

They need us to see them. *Really see them.*

Who indeed are the broken ones?

❧ 6 ❧

MALL WALKERS

Recounting an odd couple I observed as my wife and I were preparing for the birth of our first-born. A reminder that God answers all prayers but often not in the way that we expect.

After my wife's obstetrics appointment yesterday, we went mall-walking at the local Westfield Mall, attempting to coax our stubborn little baby out and into the world. My wife's ambulatory pace is somewhat hampered by an extra fifteen pounds of infant, placenta, and the other accoutrements of late pregnancy, so we slid in behind a rather unlikely couple whose pace was hampered not by pregnancy but by age.

Old age was in the form of a wizened white woman of advanced years, pace slowed by severe osteoporosis as evidenced by the "buffalo hump" that distorted her thoracic and lumbar spines. The torment of her affliction was evident in her slow, unsteady gait.

This feeble woman was accompanied, not by her husband or by any family, but by a young black woman whose abundance of hair was neatly arranged in an intricate braid which tumbled down her back, ending at the superior brim of her pelvis. From my travels with the military, I could place this young woman's accent as western African—Ghana or Senegal, perhaps. She was dressed in a traditional, brightly colored yet modest long dress that is commonly worn by women in those parts of the world.

These were two incredibly different people from very disparate backgrounds thrown together by the incredible dislocation and mobility that our modern age has to offer. They were brought together, on this very day, at the local shopping mall, of all places. Coincidence or providence? Regardless, it was a spectacle which belied all the precepts that identity politics would have us believe.

Here were two incredibly distinct people who had no business knowing each other, yet the young African woman held the other woman gently by the hand, patiently leading her along. It was a role reversal—the younger leading the older. The young African woman led the older white woman through the usual mall obstacles—unsupervised, distracted children not looking where they were going, technology addled adults who cannot be bothered to look up from their devices and so were also not looking where they were going, and kiosk hawkers aggressively peddling their beauty aids, dubiously promising eternal youth.

Listening in, I realized that the older woman had advanced dementia. She asked the same questions of her young friend repeatedly, "Why are we here? Where are we going? What is it I need from the mall again?"

The modern age, with its incessant demands for our attention and its frenetic pace, puts us in a frame of mind in which such repeated queries would be found incredibly annoying to say the least. Yet, this young woman from Africa, probably recently immigrated to our country, was clearly not yet immersed in our modern ways. In her culture, elders are respected, valued, looked after, and not consigned wholesale to the oblivion of nursing homes. In her culture, I knew that elders are kept at home and lovingly cared for, remaining with dignity as integral parts of the family. This young woman was from the old country, and I could tell.

This young woman from Africa took the woman's repeated questioning in stride, with great patience, understanding, and dare I say, love? She answered the older woman's questions with great respect and deference, as someone who esteems another very highly. The young African woman kindly replied over and over again, "We are here to get a birthday card for your great granddaughter." Repeatedly providing the same answers to the same questions, she never once showed a hint of annoyance. This put me to great shame, as I am among the most impatient of people.

The more cynical out there may say, "Well, I'm sure that young woman is a well-paid caregiver. I'm sure she gets good money for her services."

However, I think that is unfair. Seeing the natural, uncoaxed, and spontaneous kindness, patience, and respect that this young woman showed toward an elder with whom, on the surface at least, she had nothing in common would implore even the most hardened and jaded of hearts to think again.

Because money cannot buy everything. It certainly cannot purchase the love, mutual respect, and affection that clearly was present in this unlikely pairing. And clearly, this young woman was not putting on a show for the money, for there was no one present evaluating her—except for me, of course, a silent observer.

It was clear to me that there was real affection between these two. In a reversal of roles, the younger was now protecting the elder. In fact, the elder had become like an innocent child again, and the younger like a guardian angel. These two were a modern Tobias and Raphael, I realized, and the firm yet gentle handhold between the two was a thing of beauty. Their gentle handhold was a sublime thing overlooked by all the other mall walkers keen to go about their business—a small, hidden act of affection, unnoticed by a heedless world but known in the heart of God. To me, their simple grasp of one another's hands was somehow a fist shaking in protest against a world that has gone off the rails in so many respects. Truly, these were two little ones against the world.

My wife and I walked behind the odd couple from the food court near Sears, almost all the way to the other end of the mall, at Nordstrom.

As we parted from them, I heard the old woman tell her young protector, "I'm so glad you're here with me. I could never get on without you." It reminded me of what Frodo said to Sam when all hope seemed lost in the darkness of Mordor, "I am glad that you are here with me, Sam, at the end of all things."

To me, her old heart was saying, "I am glad that you are with me, my young protector, at the end of all things. God has sent you to be with me from far away so that you could be here to help on this very day. My family is not here for me, but you have been watched over as you crossed the highest seas so that you could be with me here, today, at the end of all things."

It warmed my heart.

At the end of all things, when all lights have gone out, it does not matter in what manner, or in what skin color, our salvation will come.

When we have reached the end of our rope, and life has bought us to our knees, we will ask ourselves, "What am I doing here? Where am I going, really? What is it I really need?"

When we are once more reduced to the state of helpless children, a protector will be sent, in all certainty. For is it not written, "For such as these is the Kingdom of Heaven made"? This protector, a guardian angel, will be from an unlikely place that we would never expect. For the surprises of the Lord have not come to an end! He is the Lord of surprises and journeys.

And we will say to this protector, "I am glad that you are here with me, my great friend, here at the end of all things."

But will this be mere coincidence or an act of providence?

It is for each one of us to decide in the silence of our hearts.

⋑7⋐

NEIGHBORHOOD WATCH

What is rightly to be feared?

My neighborhood has a website on which residents can post about what they perceive to be suspicious activity or any other threats to neighborhood safety. Over the years, there have been several legitimate and helpful posts in this regard on the site—and for this I am thankful for the vigilance of my neighbors. Indeed, these warning have doubtless assisted me in keeping my home and belongings secure.

However, a few days ago there was a post on the site which read, "Everyone WATCH OUT (their capitalization)! The young men wearing ties and riding bikes are about again."

I took this post seriously as I do safety-related posts on the site. I started to become anxious.

When I read this warning, I have to confess I did not know exactly to whom or what the post was referring. *Hmmm…why do I need to be wary of a guy in a nice shirt and tie riding a bike?* I asked myself repeatedly. *Is it like a* Men in Black *kind of thing?* I wondered conspiratorially. Not wanting to sound stupid, I did not reply to the post, asking about what kind of threat they were referring to, but I did file the cryptic warning into the back of my mind.

The day after I read this puzzling post, I went out running in the dazzling, clear sunshine of a brilliant late summer/early autumn days that are a blessing to partake of. As I was cooling down after my run and walking back home, I spied the aforementioned neatly dressed young men riding around on bicycles, going from house to house on my street. They were knocking on doors and handing out pamphlets.

There were two of them.

And speaking of twos, I put two and two together.

"The young men wearing ties and riding bikes" that "were about again" were, in fact, Mormon missionaries.

The object of our neighborhood fear, vigilance, and watchfulness were, in fact, these two impeccably mannered, clean cut, and well-spoken young men who had spied me walking back to my home and were now approaching me with big, friendly, and sincere smiles on their faces.

The two young men got off their bikes, greeted me, and shook my sweaty hands firmly. I noticed that neither made the effort to wipe my grime off their hands afterwards. They introduced themselves as the Mormons I had concluded they were, then eagerly and politely engaged me in conversation.

I informed them that I am a practicing Catholic, and though my faith was not perfect, I was very content with it. They graciously accommodated me and made no further attempts at religious conversion or evangelization. At no point was I ever uncomfortable around these two polite, clean-cut, respectful, and well-spoken young men.

My conversation with these two was a refreshing reminder of how citizens can disagree but still be civil.

I proceeded to tell them that many of the friends that I served with in the military were Mormon. I told these two young men that I admired how calm, mature, self-assured, and just plain "d**n interesting" (they blushed at my mild expletive) my Mormon friends always were. These attributes were doubtless imparted to them by the very same arduous two-year missions that these two were currently undertaking.

I told these young men how amazed I was by the worldliness and language skills of my Mormon friends—again the result of their missionary work. A close Mormon friend of mine, a six-foot three, lily-white boy with a mustache from Utah ("Salt of the Earth, straight from the bosom of the Mormon Church," as Nanci Griffith sang) floored me when I first heard him belt out fluent Japanese when we were stationed in Okinawa together. You should have seen how the Japanese themselves reacted when they found out that this "gaijin" white boy had understood them all along. And how, as Mormons are wont to do, my friend was always self-effacing and humble about his abilities.

The two young men, who thought I was an unbeliever, listened with rapt attention to my tales of Mormon exceptionalism told with great sincerity on my part because I believed every word of it.

Finally, I told these two young men how much I admired what they were doing—leaving everything they knew and loved in order to serve something bigger than themselves. I told them to look after each other. As an emergency physician and veteran I knew what a dark place this world can be. I paraphrased scripture for them: "You guys have to be as innocent as lambs, but as cunning as snakes!" They got a good laugh from that.

Yes, the world can be a dark place, and I complimented them for their attempt to bring some much-needed light and fellowship into it. I told the two of them that I admired the fact that they were undergoing this rite of passage into adulthood—for true rights of initiation and passage for the young have fallen into disuse and neglect in our country—with the unfortunate consequence that many adults are truly little better than overgrown, self-absorbed adolescents.

Then we shook hands and parted as friends.

The Mormons got back on their bikes and rode on.

I walked home and thought about the post on our neighborhood website.

These Mormon youngsters—that's what they were, really just kids—we are supposed to be wary and suspicious of them as we would be of the neighborhood stalker or Peeping Tom? Are we supposed to equate these two polite, well-spoken, well-dressed, clean-cut, and God-fearing young men who don't even ask for money, mind you, to the possible perpetrators of home invasions or car thefts?

Surely, the person who posted that warning must have been joking.

But sadly and soberly I realized that no, the poster was probably not joking. There was no reason for me to doubt that the post had been made in all seriousness, as all other posts on the site had been. My Mormon missionary friends were somehow considered legitimate threats to neighborhood peace and security.

Hardly surprising, I realized, as I thought about it more and more. We have become a society that sensationalizes trivialities and trivializes what are probably the most pressing and profound matters of our time. We conjure threats where they do not exist and conveniently ignore and overlook evils that we see taking place in our everyday lives. We teach our children to be afraid of this, and afraid of that—but are we teaching them to fear the proper "threats"?

To be afraid of two Mormon guys on their missions?

Is Mormonism now the menace of our times?

We perceive as threatening the two young men who seek only to spread the Word of a loving God as they see it and offer fellowship to a society so desperately in need of comfort. Yet we do not think twice when confronted with the deep affronts to human dignity, freedom, and rights that we see playing out on our television screens every day.

Evil has become banal.

Even more worrisome is what all that is true beauty, light, love, and truth have become; at best, more obscure and increasingly difficult to discern, and at worst, intentionally degraded and viciously slandered and sullied by those with agendas and special interests.

Let's hope that beauty, light, love, and truth don't become banal as well. For we live in very strange times.

However, the truth is that we need more clean cut, polite, well-dressed, well-spoken, friendly, and God-fearing young people to invade our neighborhoods.

You go, Mormon dudes!

Cunning as serpents.

But innocent as lambs.

We need more like you.

❧ 8 ❧

War Machines

The greatest battles are fought within. The greatest enemy you will ever confront may well be yourself.

I went to see the movie *American Sniper* when it was released. The theater was surprisingly full. As Bradley Cooper, playing SEAL sniper Chris Kyle, makes the kill shot that serves as the film's denouement, the crowd actually cheered—something that I have not heard at a cinema in a long time. Honestly, as a veteran, I did not know whether I should be heartened or dismayed by the cheering; my own feelings were deeply ambivalent. This is because I was able to watch most of the crowd file in before the film started, and the majority were affluent and young, well-heeled, yuppified-types who I would venture to guess had probably never spent a day in uniform. Yet, they actually *cheered*.

As a veteran and a physician, I am intimately and unfortunately acquainted with human demise. I know that death indelibly affects not only the deceased, of course, but also family, friends, and the entire community. As a veteran who has served with Marine infantry, I am profoundly aware of the hidden wounds and torment that dealing out death has had on the *killers* themselves. In my nearly four years of service with the infantry, I never met a single Marine who relished or was

59

truly proud of the fact that he ended the life of another human being, despite all the bluster and seeming bravado. Quite the contrary, actually.

Hence my deep misgivings as the audience cheered when Chris Kyle made the superhuman kill shot, which of course played out in explicit, almost pornographic slow motion. To be frank, all of the jubilation disgusted me. To me, what it all amounted to was detached, thrill-seeking civilians seeking distraction in a few hours of military voyeurism.

Disgusting.

One of the folks I had seen walk in to also watch *American Sniper* was an older gentleman. He was conspicuous because he stuck out like the proverbial sore thumb in the otherwise young, over-caffeinated, smartphone-toting crowd. He had a "Vietnam Veteran" cap on over his long grey hair and wore the leathers of a Harley guy. On his jacket, he had a patch of the ribbon that goes with the Bronze Star medal. He sat a row ahead of me, a few seats down. I watched him as everyone else cheered the kill shot and noticed that Mr. Vietnam Vet just sat there. He did not cheer but rather looked disbelievingly around him as the crowd whooped and hollered about the superhuman SEAL sniper kill shot. Mr. Vietnam Vet then shook his head resignedly and, with a sorrowful expression on his face, sank down further into his seat.

That confirmed for me that he was not a poseur; he was the real deal.

Because veterans know the reality of war.

Veterans know that war is brutal and cruel. War is grim. War is ugly and cannot be refined. Veterans know that ultimately war is not glorious, but that the true meaning of war is sacrifice and loss.

And veterans know that nobody really cheers during or after a firefight—instead you pick up the pieces and do your utmost to strengthen that which remains. There is no cheering after a firefight. After the adrenaline rush wears off, you are instead overcome by a wave of fear, nausea, restlessness, hypervigilance, and dread because you know that the future has more of the same in store. And in retrospect, we veterans realize that this toxic mix of troubled emotions served as the basis for the Post Traumatic Stress Disorder (PTSD) that many of us continue to grapple with, decades after we left active duty.

As the end credits rolled and real footage of Chris Kyle's funeral was shown on the screen, Mr. Vietnam Vet *did* react. I saw this older man lift his glasses up and dry his eyes. I could not blame him, since I needed to do the same.

As rousing and realistic as the action sequences in the film were, I felt that *American Sniper* was most accurate and powerful in its riveting recounting of Mr. Kyle's difficulties when trying to adjust back to civilian life—when he struggled with PTSD. Bradley Cooper's portrayal of Kyle's guilt over *killing*, detachment from his loved ones, anger, inability to just "let it go," resentment, disillusionment with, and general isolation from the rest of American society was right on. Bradley Cooper's portrayal of a maladjusted, mentally frayed, and on-the-edge Chris Kyle is, indeed, an accurate portrayal of what many veterans today continue to struggle with in their daily lives.

Anyone who has been in harm's way for our nation will be able to identify with these feelings. Many of us have realized that perhaps the most difficult of all deployments is, in fact, that final deployment which brings us "home" once more.

Sadly, many find truth in the adage of *"you can't go home again."* This is not because "home" has changed but because *you* have and, in some ways, not for the better.

I did feel like cheering during the film—but not until the very end, when Chris Kyle finally puts his demons to rest, reconciles with his family and his countrymen, and proceeds to go on with his life as a contributing member of society. To me, and I would like to think for the old Vietnam vet, *that* is more cheer-worthy than some unlikely kill shot from a mile out.

I think that the lesson of *American Sniper* is that while our military can overcome tremendous adversity and perform amazing but true feats of heroism and sacrifice, in reality, we are just fallible, flawed, and sometimes very weak human beings. We are also your fathers and mothers, sisters and brothers, cousins and friends, and the boy or girl who lives a few houses down the street. We are even your doctor sometimes. We are not all superhuman SEAL snipers. We think. We feel. And many of us continue to hurt badly and need your help and understanding.

Because there are men inside those war machines.

❧9❧

COMMUNICATION BREAKDOWN

Hearing and listening—like knowledge and wisdom—are two very different things.

I was working an evening shift in the emergency department recently. Evenings—that time after dinner and before midnight—are usually the busiest time of the day in our little emergency department world, and that day was no different. I was humping it (seeing lots of patients indeed, let me tell you), dispensing diagnoses, weighing risk/benefit rations, assessing pre-test probabilities, rendering reassurance, and sometimes, breaking bad news in a "belt fed" fashion, as the Marines say.

I was in my zone; and when I'm in the zone, efficiency and productivity mean *everything*.

When I walked into a room to see the next patient, I saw the nurse talking on her phone and pressing buttons repeatedly on a laptop. She looked very irritated.

I asked, "What's wrong?"

"This patient is deaf," the nurse replied, "And I can't get the laptop we use to contact the sign language interpreter to work. I'm on the phone with IT right now. . .but nothing is working." The nurse looked at me, rolled her eyes, and gave an exasperated sigh. And so did the patient. Understandably she gave an exasperated sigh too as she watched the nurse fumbling hopelessly with the malfunctioning laptop, now rendered useless due to a glitch with the vaunted technology with which we insist on impressing ourselves.

The patient and I then eyed each other warily across the invisible, yet seemingly insurmountable and noiseless chasm of silence that separated her from me. We sensed an interaction that would be fraught with the difficulty that accompanies a breakdown in communication. I waited a few moments more to see if the nurse—trying diligently and valiantly, as all our nurses do—could resolve the issue with the laptop.

My impatience got the best of me. Flustered, I stormed out of the room, arms akimbo, shaking my head, and cursing the emergency room gods who afflicted me with dysfunctional technology at this, the busiest part of our day. I walked to the printer and took some paper out of the tray; next, I ambled over to the rack to grab a clipboard; then I borrowed a pen from the clerk because I am always losing pens, it seems.

I was not pleased. But in the military, we were taught to improvise and be resourceful. To make do with less. . .

So, *No laptop?* I thought. *We're doing this old school then. With pen and paper!*

Yep. Pen and paper. It was 2018, and technological unreliability had propelled me back to the age of handwritten communication, manual typewriters, snail mail, and analog technology. A part of me even started looking for one of those old phones with a rotary dial.

"Well, so much for efficiency and productivity!" I muttered to myself cynically.

I walked back to the patient's room. She lay in her bed, the mirror image of what I must have looked like just a few moments ago—arms akimbo, head shaking, with a highly dissatisfied look on her face. The nurse was still, to her credit, trying to get the laptop to work; but it just sat there, its useless monitor staring at us stupidly like the cyclopean eye of a detached, impassive, and long dead god, no longer worthy of worship.

I told the nurse, "I've got this. Don't worry about the laptop. We're going to do this the old school way," showing her the clipboard, pen, and paper. She smiled at me, laughed understandingly, then left to triage yet more patients.

You can't imagine the depth of my perturbation at that point! It was busy. Patients with undifferentiated complaints and problems were piling up in the ER and the waiting room. And here I was, stuck with pen, clipboard, and paper in hand, like Jimmy Olson, cub reporter for the *Daily Planet*, from the 1950s "Superman" comic strip.

I took a deep breath. "Try and be patient," I told myself. "It'll be OK."

Then I wrote out, in all caps on the sheet of paper: "HELLO, MY NAME IS DR. VILLARUZ. HOW CAN I HELP?" then handed her the clipboard.

She looked at the clipboard, then at me, disbelievingly, the expression on her face saying, "You've got to be freakin' kidding me, right?!"

But then I saw her close her eyes, take a deep breath as I had just done, and with a resigned look on her face, she took the clipboard and pen from me. She proceeded to write out her response.

She wrote out the basics of her chief complaint. *Fair enough*, I thought. *We're making progress!*

In painfully slow and tedious longhand, I proceeded to tease out the specifics of her problem. "DOES ANYTHING MAKE IT BETTER OR WORSE?" I wrote. "DOES IT COME AND GO? OR IS IT ALWAYS THERE?" I put it as plainly as possible, of course. We're taught in medical school, rightly or not, to assume that your patient only completed a primary education, and to patronizingly dumb down our interrogatives accordingly.

It took her a while to write out her response, which I did not expect. I was only looking forward to a primary school kind of response.

What she wrote back to me took me by complete surprise. Yes, I was not expecting this. I was surprised but pleasantly so.

Her response was a paragraph in length. It was filled with polysyllabic, complex graduate level words like "EXACERBATED," "ALLEVIATED," "WAXING," "WANING," "SENSITIVITY," and "INTERMITTENT" all put together in a grammatically irreproachable, almost lyrical fashion, replete with proper spelling and punctuation.

Now, I love to read. And as anybody who reads my writings regularly knows, I love to write. I'm a total stickler for proper grammar. However, even more I love fine language, the hidden subtleties behind the meaning of words, the satisfaction that comes with finding a descriptor that is just right, the power of metaphors, and the poetic grandeur of a phrase perfectly put together.

Language is an art to me. I appreciate its power. For language transcends our mere senses. Words can be *felt* by our souls at the deepest level of our being. Oh yes, words have power...and if properly employed can hit with all the undeniable impact of a 7.62mm round to the chest.

As a lover of language, I drank in this patient's response as one would water in the desert. Her response was a real pleasure to take in, and her words left me smiling. It was a nice break from the almost guttural, mono-syllabic responses I usually get not just from patients but from most people in modern life. They bought me back to, were reminiscent of, and had the 7.62mm hitting power of the high language I'd read in the witty conversations in Jane Austen's novels, in American Revolutionary and Civil War correspondence, the poetry of Yeats, or in Tolkien's description of the great beauty of Luthien in *The Silmarillion*. Yes, like water in parched wastes were her words—a real treat for me.

It is said that when one of our senses atrophies, is compromised, or is taken from us, the other faculties and senses grow more acute and adept in order to compensate. This was definitely true in this young woman's case. Living in the isolation of her silent world had caused her powers of written expression, her literate skills, to magnify and wax wonderful and sublime.

Her disability, which many would construe to be a calamitous misfortune, was in reality a great gift and blessing. She was now favored with an amazing faculty for grammar, subtlety of meaning, and just plain *beauty* in her written skills that we, her more aurally adept fellow humans, will probably never achieve. And after experiencing the power of this young woman's words, I felt uniquely privileged indeed at having had the chance to share in her world of soundless grandeur if only for a few moments.

This amazing epiphany was made possible by a laptop not working that day.

At that moment, several realizations went through my consciousness.

One of them was an article of faith that my grandmother

used to always reminded me of: "Al, only God can create good from evil and misfortune."

I realized that this young woman's disability was, in reality, a great boon and blessing from God. Our Creator had transformed her affliction into an asset.

Another realization was: "If that laptop was working, and I was being efficient and productive as I always like to be, I likely would never have beheld this young woman's hidden gifts. I never would have been honored with this privileged insight into her silent but unexpectedly profound and rich world."

In our age of email, Skype, and text messaging, we pride ourselves on our abilities of instantaneous communication. Yes, we have immediate contact, but are we really communicating? We have a never-ending desire for yet more speed, efficiency, bandwidth, and productivity, but that does come at a cost. What subtleties, what depth of feeling, hidden meanings, nuances, what profound sharing of affection and feeling— indeed, what *beauty*—do we miss out on in all this desire for even more efficiency and speed?

We just don't think we ever have the time to take a phone call from an old friend and have an actual conversation. We are too busy to write a snail mail letter to a distant relative, send a condolence card to a grieving friend, or are too otherwise occupied to drive in order to see an elderly parent and truly be physically available and present for them?

What do we miss out on in our endless and very American quest for ever more efficiency, productivity, and speed?

Is there a real cost to all of this convenience that we cannot always readily perceive?

A few months before my dad passed away, I was having dinner with him and my mom at their home. During the course of the meal, Mom stopped eating and picked up her tablet in order to find something on Facebook she wanted to share with us. While waiting for her, I absentmindedly picked up my phone to return a text message from a friend. This, of course, left Dad ignored and overlooked. In that moment, he became a virtual non-entity as Mom and I indulged ourselves with our devices.

Dad shook the both of us out of our electronic reverie by saying something I'll never forget. He said thoughtfully, with a hint of bitterness, "You know, what all of these electronics really do is bring distant relatives closer at the expense of making closer relatives more distant."

Now I will never know if Dad thought that up himself or read it somewhere, but his powerful and very valid observation had again all of the effect of another 7.62 round to the chest. The truth of his utterance led my mom and I to put down our electronic adult pacifiers like children who had just been rightfully chastened by an admonishing parent. Because we knew in our hearts that my old man was right.

These devices, which are supposed to make our lives so much more convenient and easier, have the insidious side effect of taking us out of the beauty of the moment. Now, in retrospect, I realize it was one of the last meals I would share with my father. These devices have the perilous consequence of robbing the present of its power, of tragically removing us from the exquisite immediacy of that which is present before us in the here and now, and of obscuring the beauty of that which is before our very eyes *at this very moment*.

In reality, we pay a very high price for all of this convenience, efficiency, productivity, and speed. Perhaps the laptops need to go off-line or malfunction with more frequency.

Now, back to my deaf patient.

The workup completed, I returned to her bedside. Fortunately, her tests revealed that nothing life threatening or otherwise unfortunate was going on with her. Reverting back to the ancient, but not necessarily inferior, form of communication that we had been reduced to, I picked up pen and paper and wrote out:

"SORRY IT TOOK SO LONG. I HAVE GOOD NEWS. ALL OF YOUR TESTS ARE NEGATIVE. LOOKS LIKE YOU'RE GOING TO BE OK."

I proceeded to give her smile and an effusive thumbs up. She smiled back, then I handed her the pen and paper.

The patient began to write out: "DR. VILLARUZ, WORDS CANNOT EXPRESS THE FATHOMLESS DEPTH OF MY SINCERE AND HEARTFELT GRATITUDE FOR WHAT YOU AND YOUR STAFF HAVE DONE FOR ME."

Sincere. Fathomless. Gratitude...WOW! I thought to myself as I read out her response. And more words like "consolation," "tranquility," and most importantly, "unbridled happiness."

Yes. Like water in the desert were her words. I felt like I was conversing with Lizzie from Jane Austen's *Pride and Prejudice*.

But she also had written, "Words cannot express." *How very true*, I thought. Words cannot express. We are immersed with and beguiled by all of this vaunted technology that we try and impress ourselves with, devices that fill our lives and consciousness with an endless stream of words and images, words upon words. It's a perpetual, never-ending stream of information. Words, endless words, words upon words fill our lives. A 24/7/365 barrage of cable news and social media.

However, does all of this information overload really do much to improve our existence? Do all of these words do much to truly improve the human condition? I don't think so. "Words are not enough," my deaf patient had written. Words are not enough! All of this information! However, in the end, words—mere information—are not enough because knowledge and wisdom are two very different things, are they not?

No. Words are not enough.

All of this technology. . .it is not enough.

Indeed, it was an interruption in this torrent of information and tech—this communication breakdown, this *inconvenience*—that had the paradoxical effect of allowing me to communicate on a deeper, more profound and intimate level with this patient. A breakdown with the vaunted technology that supposedly makes our lives so much better instead forced us to improvise and use a mode of communication that was older, and yes, less convenient but more tried and true, more intimate and profound to shatter forever the barrier of silence which had separated us.

Handwritten words, written after proper consideration, reflection, and thought were not as clumsy or random as text speech, written in a rush to be even more efficient. These handwritten words had the hitting power of a 7.62 round, almost forgotten, certainly neglected, like "the Deep Magic from before the Beginning of Time" that C.S. Lewis wrote about in his Narnia books. They are an archaic, outmoded form of communication, certainly more inconvenient and time consuming.

But that is just it, is it not?

We were able to communicate more effectively, deeply, profoundly—breaking through the barrier of silence and misunderstanding separating us—because we took the time.

Because we *took* the *time*.

So much for the allure of speed and efficiency.

What new worlds, what new insights, what wonderful discoveries—indeed, what sublime beauty—would become available to us if we only took the time?

But is it really "The Deep Magic from before the Beginning of Time"?

Yes, indeed. I believe so. Truly. Deep, timeless magic that can still hit like a 7.62mm round to the chest.

And with that, the patient wrote out, "THANK YOU, DR. VILLARUZ!"

Then she blew me a kiss in gratitude, which, a friend of mine who knows sign language later told me is one of the highest of compliments.

Never had a patient do that before!

All this. . .just because we took the time. . .and allowed ourselves to undergo a little inconvenience, a slight delay, an annoying inefficiency.

For we lose much when we multitask, we sacrifice untold beauty for the sake of speed, close ourselves off for the sake of convenience, and perhaps even end up doing evil in the name of efficiency.

We lose out on a lot in life when we forget that God can still make good from evil, conjure beauty from an unpleasant situation, and engineer hope in the midst of an apparent inconvenience.

We lose out on much when we do not take the time.

We lose out on much when we forget that the singular moments of our busy lives are fleeting, passing, unique. . .and never will come again.

➤ 10 ❖

HOMICIDAL

Real men are an endangered species.

A few months ago, I took care of a patient whose chief complaint on the emergency department (ED) tracking board read, ominously enough, "HOMICIDAL." I took note of the patient's age and gender. Turns out that he was a boy in his mid-teens. Seeing these demographics, I automatically assumed that this boy was yet another sad product of the indiscriminate and reckless lockdowns of the last few years, a forced isolation that has ravaged fragile young psyches and sent the rates of mental illness and suicides through the roof among children and adolescents.

"Here we go again." I sighed to myself resignedly as I went to go see this young boy.

On my way to his room, I encountered the Sheriff's deputy who had brought the boy into the emergency department. He was filling out the boy's emergency petition, with a world-weary look on his face, a tired expression tinged with sadness. I asked him for some background regarding the patient. He proceeded to recount the events which led to the boy being bought into the ED.

"We get called over to his house all the time, Doc. Domestic violence kind of stuff, you know? Kid's mom is shacked up with her boyfriend. Boyfriend gets drunk; they fight; he beats the mom. Get the picture? This kid has a sister as well. Real dad, biological dad is out of the picture. . ." He shook his head knowingly during the last sentence.

At this point I interrupted the deputy, asking, "If you guys get called over there all the time, why did you bring the boy in today?"

(I didn't think of it at that moment, but perhaps a better question would have been, "How come you bought the boy here instead of arresting the mom's boyfriend for assault?")

The deputy answered me, point blank, "Because this time, the kid threatened to kill the boyfriend. Threatened to stab him. Old boyfriend got spooked and called us."

"Hence, the HOMICIDAL in all caps, I see on our tracker, deputy?"

"Yep!" the deputy replied matter of factly, eager as he was to finish his tedious paperwork.

I thanked the deputy for his time and went to go see the patient.

He was in one of our bare and unadorned psychiatric rooms. Not quite a padded cell, it was nonetheless stripped of any cords, medical equipment, and monitors that psychiatric patients could potentially use to harm themselves or others. The boy had already been relieved of his street clothes, which he also could use to hurt himself, and was made to wear our humiliating paper blue scrubs, the tell-tale sign of a patient in the ED for a behavioral health problem.

The boy was clean cut, I noted. His scrub top was even neatly tucked into his bottoms. I had already been through his medical records and knew that he had no history of aberrant or anti-social behavior. Also, the deputy had confirmed that the boy had no record of misconduct, so I did not think his benign appearance was strange in any way. He sat in the bed quietly, arms akimbo, head upright, and looked me in the eye, face not buried in a cellphone, as I walked into the room to see him. *Seems more engaged than his peers,* I thought to myself.

Seeing a full specimen cup on the counter, I also realized with some surprise and satisfaction that he had already obediently provided the urine specimen that the triage nurse had requested earlier. This is no small feat, as coaxing a urine out of a behavioral health patient is one of the greatest trials we must overcome in our little ED world.

Not at all what I was expecting.

My first impression of this child was not of a homicidal killer. Nope. His spotless record indicated that this boy was probably quite sane. In fact, this child, to me, on initial impression at least, seemed to have his act more together than most teens in his age range.

I introduced myself.

He told me his name and called me "Sir."

Then I got down to taking a history. He related the chaotic tale of his life so far, a tale told with sad frequency. His biological father bailed when he was in grade school. His mother, sister, and he have since lived with a rogue's gallery succession of his mother's boyfriends. Boyfriend du jeur was into drinking, doing drugs, and taking out his frustrations on his mother. The boy also did not like how the boyfriend sometimes touched his sister, and on and on.

The boy then recounted the details of today's assault on his mother. At describing the beating of the one who had given him life, the one who nursed him and comforted him when he was distressed for as long as he could remember, his admirable composure broke, and he began to sob, the tears flowing like a river down his cheeks and staining his scrubs to a darker shade of blue.

"You can stop, you don't have to tell me anymore," I said to him, putting a fatherly hand on his shoulder. I had to remind myself that as mature and strong as this boy seemed initially, at his core, he still was a *child*—a child that had seen too much. . .a child that had seen what no child should ever see.

The boy went on, though, feeling he had found a sympathetic ear. He said, "It's just that when I saw him hitting my mom this time and pushing my sister around, I just wanted to protect the both of them *more than anything*. I got a knife from the kitchen and told **** that I would stab him to death if he hurt my mom and sister anymore. I told him I would KILL HIM. If my mom hadn't told me to stop, I would have killed him."

Homicidal.

And he cried. There were tears, but his eyes held my gaze, almost defiantly. There were tears, yes. But as the boy stared defiantly ahead, in his eyes I saw the precocity of absolute, fierce, undeniable, and unwavering conviction—irresistible, carrying away all before it.

Yes. He would kill. He would *kill* to protect those he loved most. To me, two convictions resounded most in his gripping testimony: first, he loved his mother and sister more than words could say; and second, that he would do *anything* to protect them.

He cried. The boy stammered and cried. He looked pathetic in his blue scrubs. But in his eyes remained that terrible look of determination and one-hundred percent commitment to love and protect. To me, he was transformed. He was no longer one of a nameless legion of fatherless boys. He was no longer the forlorn, lost, and sad product of an off-the-rails society that has lost its direction in far too many ways.

No.

The defiant and determined look in his eyes told me that this patient was no child.

He was a lion.

This boy was the embodiment of all that is noble, desirable, and sought-after in a man—namely assertiveness, courage, protectiveness, selflessness, and strength. *Honor* as well. This patient was not a boy. Today, in displaying the very natural instinct of protecting his kin, he had become a man.

No, not a man.

He was a lion.

He was a king. For kings banish and destroy the beasts of chaos and evil that threaten the realm.

Furthermore, in a society where initiation and meaningful coming-of-age rites are woefully lacking, being able to remain on your parent's health insurance until your late twenties is somehow perceived as a societal triumph, where de facto childhood seems to persist interminably, and young adults fail to launch with alarmingly regularity, this boy had outdone his seemingly more advantaged peers and made the difficult transition into real adulthood.

He had become a man.

Looking at him, I did not see another wayward, basket case product of a confused and unhinged world. Instead, I saw a young Zulu warrior who had dispatched the leopard that was terrorizing his village and was now worthy to present himself as a warrior to the great king, Shaka-Zulu. I saw a young Sioux brave who had counted coup with his first enemy—demonstrating that killing and victory were not the same—earning the right to wear an eagle feather in his braid and join the lodge of the great Crazy Horse.

This boy had been initiated that day and undergone an increasingly neglected rite of passage.

That day, he had become a man.

Lest it get too unpredictable and while I tried to maintain some degree of clinical detachment and objectivity, I gently ended the interview there. As much as I felt for this young man, the ever-present emergency physician in me knew that there were other patients I had to see and soon. I continued to grasp his shoulder and reassured him that if he continued to cooperate, we would come to a resolution of this matter as quickly as possible...that we the people society turns to when all lights had gone out, and they have nowhere else to run, would get him the help he needed.

But help?

Real help?

What kind of help are we going to get this kid? I mean, really? I asked myself knowingly and cynically, walking back to my workstation to do some documentation. *What help for this kid, really?* I asked myself sadly, for the jaded, world-weary, and fatalistic part of me that has been doing this for far too long knew all too well what awaited this boy—or more appropriately, I reminded myself—this young *man*.

I knew that he would be involuntarily committed to spend time in a psychiatric facility for the disorder of loving his mother and sister. I knew that there was no way he would be allowed back home unless his mother got her act together and mustered up the moral fiber to dump the boyfriend, so for the psychopathology of very naturally wanting to protect those he loved most, he would be anonymously consigned to the oblivion of a dysfunctional, sclerotic, state-run foster care system.

And that is what happened to this young *man*.

That's what happened to this young lion.

That's what happened to this hidden king.

As a professional, I have no choice but to file away such sorrowful episodes into a mental bottom drawer if I have any hope of maintaining my sanity and hence, my already fraying emotional longevity as an emergency physician. However, the questions that this case brought up ate away at my intellect and conscience. Questions like, What is worth fighting for? What in life is worth the last full measure of our devotion? What indeed is worth dying for? And what, if anything, could possibly be worth *killing for*?"

The ramifications of this young man's eventual fate were also deeply troubling for me. Here we had a young man, by all indications perfectly sane and in his right mind, being consigned to the funny farm for being the personification of what has been, for untold millennia, all that is desirable in a man—strength, courage, selflessness, decisiveness, and protectiveness.

Here was a young man that would be forever stigmatized by a psychiatric diagnosis, limiting his ability to do almost anything in life—from finding work, getting into the right school, to buying a firearm—for displaying the evolutionarily desirable and completely natural characteristics that have ensured our survival as a species for untold ages.

Here we had a young man who was being marginalized to the fringes of our fraying society for being...*a man*.

And I am telling the truth when I say that I lie awake at night, fearful of what this young man's fate may portend for my own sons.

For there can be no doubt, we are living in a society with increasingly disordered priorities. Every day we are confronted with a value system that through our own disinterest, distraction, and neglect has inexorably become perverse, dystopic, and distorted. We have become a society that brands a young man as psychiatrically ill for quite simply being a *man*.

Instances of these misplaced priorities and disordered values have multiplied at an alarming rate, more so it seems in the last few nightmarish years.

You could see it during COVID, when the economy crashed, leading to lost jobs and income. This led to food handouts reminiscent of the bread lines and soup kitchens of the Great Depression. What was inexplicable, to me at least, was watching the news and seeing some folks drive up to the food banks in a Lexus or a Mercedes. The sight of this floored me. When did making a car payment become more important than putting food on the table?

You see it on our southern border. Why do we spend billions to safeguard the frontiers of corrupt foreign nations like Ukraine while offering no resistance whatsoever to the millions who have surreptitiously violated our own frontiers and entered our own country illegally since 2021? These millions will be competing with established citizens and taxpayers for resources that are steadily dwindling.

You saw it at the Uvalde school shooting. Heavily armed and armored cops nonchalantly checking their cell phones and using hand-sanitizer with all the banal indifference of ho-hum "just another day at the office," while several meters down the hall could be heard the faint but unmistakable pop-pop-pop of 5.56mm AR rounds being discharged. . .each pop marking the end of a young life which had only barely begun.

We emphasize esoterica, publicly parsing out the nuances of pronouns and deeply private matters like whom we choose to share our beds with while our interstates literally collapse around us, and air travel, once so safe, reliable, and predictable, becomes a roll of the dice.

We sit, enthralled by our technology, addicted to the god-like feeling of control we believe it gives us over our lives, immersing ourselves in never-ending ever more fantastical, vulgar, and mind-numbing streaming entertainment, while the reality is our supply chain is crumbling around us, basic necessities go on back-order, and our medical, transportation, and law enforcement infrastructures are taxed to the limit and are on the very brink of failure.

We remember the name of the bartender on the last cruise we took but forget the names of the nurses and doctor who saved the life of our child when she was desperately ill.

We fancy ourselves as forward-thinking, progressive, and sophisticated, but nonetheless conclude that a boy must be mentally ill for the audacity of wanting to protect, to the point of homicide, those he loves the most in this life.

But what is worth fighting for? What is worth dying for? What is worth sacrificing oneself for? What, God forbid, is worth killing for? That child. . .no check that. . .that young man clearly knew the answer to that more clearly, more fiercely, and with more conviction than those who saw fit to judge him.

In a culture that has become increasingly milquetoast, politically correct, and non-confrontational, few have the moral courage to even ask, much less answer, these stark questions. However, unlike the mostly frivolous and trifling First World inconsistencies and dilemmas enumerated thus far, in the answer to these profound existentialist choices, there should be no ambiguity whatsoever.

There *are* some causes in life worth fighting for. Some matters worth dying for. . . And there are some loved ones in our lives that just may be worth killing for.

And that young man? He certainly did nothing to warrant being involuntarily placed in a psychiatric facility.

Rather, as the Marines whom I served with used to say when they witnessed truly courageous, exemplary, noble, or selfless behavior: "I'd give that kid a medal!"

❧ 11 ❧

THE MOST IMPORTANT THING

A Jewish man who bore witness to the greatest evils of the twentieth century once taught me much about hope, courage, human goodness, and perseverance. He also reminded me that paranoia can be justifiable.

When I was a medical student at the University of Chicago, one of the professors of psychiatry who instructed me was a man named Dr. G. who remains one of the most deeply influential people I have ever met in my life.

Dr. G. was one of a handful of holocaust survivors on a faculty dominated by Jews and was, as a result, treated deferentially by his peers and accorded a special level of respect. Dr. G. was a Polish Jew, and as a teen, had been imprisoned in a Nazi concentration camp in the eastern part of his home country. I recall that it was not one the larger camps like Auschwitz or Buchenwald but one of the outlying, less well-known death factories. He was saved at the last possible moment when the Red Army expelled the Nazis from the part of eastern Poland where his camp was situated, granting him deliverance from the gas chambers.

Astutely sensing that one murderous, totalitarian regime was merely being traded for yet another, Dr. G. was somehow able to escape eastern Europe before the Iron Curtain fell. He ended up in South Africa, of all places, where he studied to become a physician.

When the apartheid policies of the Afrikaner regime became too much for him to stomach, he eventually emigrated to the United States in the early 70s. However, there was one Afrikaner peculiarity that Dr. G. brought with him from his days in South Africa. Whenever he wanted to emphasize a point he was making, he would always punctuate it with "hey" at the end. If you were male, the "hey" would often be accompanied by a fatherly jab into your arm, as if to emphasize his point even further.

It is remarkable that in a mere twenty-five years, Dr. G. had already fled and been victimized by oppressive regimes *three* times in his existence. Remarkable indeed, but then again, Dr. G. was a remarkable man.

Professor G. was tall and very thin. He always wore a Jewish *kippah*. Emaciated-looking, almost skeletal, with a long, thin, leonine face, and sunken eyes, he looked as if he were still being tormented and deprived in the camps he had survived as a teen. One of our professors once said of him, rather uncharitably, "Dr. G. looks more like a pathologist than a proper psychiatrist!"

Dr. G.'s foreboding appearance concealed a generous, kind, patient, outgoing, and sensitive heart. He was brilliant, dual boarded in adult and child psychiatry, so I worked with Dr. G. not only during my psychiatric clerkship but also when I rotated through the pediatric oncology service later on during my third-year clerkships.

Here, Dr. G. saw to the emotional needs of children and parents who had been brought to the end of their emotional tethers by cancer and the very real possibility of mortality. These children and their families were literally holding on by a thread, medically and psychologically.

And into this emotionally charged, seemingly hopeless milieu strode six-foot four, thin, gaunt appearing Dr. G. I remember children in particular being taken aback when they saw Dr. G.'s tortured, imposing frame enter their rooms, but he would quickly disarm them by squatting down to their level—no easy thing for a man already in his late 60s—so he would not seem so threatening. He would then smile and always introduce himself like this:

"Hello, I'm Dr. G. Do you know what else starts with a G? Giraffe starts with a G! You can call me Dr. Giraffe too, because I'm tall like a giraffe!"

At this point, with a big grin and lots of goofy theatricality that only a child would understand, Dr. G. would slowly stand, extending to the full extent of his six-foot four frame and raise his hands over his head.

"See—tall! Like a giraffe!"

"Dr. Giraffe, Dr. Giraffe!" the children would invariably say in response, laughing with glee at his play acting. And thus, the doctor-patient relationship was quickly established!

Because Dr. G., you see, despite all of the suffering and travails he had experienced in his life, never lost his compassion, empathy, and generosity. He never lost his childlike sense of wonder at even the simplest occurrences, and as a result, he could relate easily with the very young. His trials never shrunk his heart; it was so large that he continued to welcome these little ones, seemingly bereft of hope, into it as well. Because if there was one thing that Dr. G.'s past had taught him, it was that one should never give up hope, even when all seemed lost—even as the gas-chambers and ovens had once beckoned. Dr. G. offered a vision of hope and consolation at a time when all lights had seemed to have gone out for families on the oncology ward. He was a witness to the possibility of an amazing and saving grace in situations that seemed hopeless.

And everyone loved him for it.

I recall that unlike some of his august peers who simply could not be bothered, Dr. G. shared a rapport and easy relationship with the African American ladies who ran the cafeteria and food service, and with the African American and Hispanic men on the janitorial staff. I would often see him making the cafeteria ladies laugh with earthy, irreverent comments, usually directed at hospital administration. I remember them saying to him through their laughter, "Dr. G., you crazy!" Because he was one of the few faculty who did not think them unworthy of attention, these very thoughtful ladies made special kosher lunches for Dr. G. in return. I always thought that this was a very kind gesture on their part.

With the men of the janitorial staff, Dr. G. could often be spied whispering conspiratorially in the hallways with a wry grin on his face, probably sharing humor of a more off-color and ribald variety. He would leave them guffawing, slapping their knees with hilarity, and saying loudly something along the lines of "Now, Doc, that's funny!"

The other professors looked down their noses at what they thought was Dr G.'s fraternization with "the help," but Old Man G. could care less what they thought, hey?

I wondered myself at how an eastern European Jew could have such an easy familiarity with these folks of color from the other side of the world, but I eventually realized that it was because they, like Dr. G., had been discriminated against, downtrodden, marginalized, persecuted, or silenced by the ruling establishment during their lives. Dr. G. was a holocaust survivor who had also experienced apartheid in South Africa, a way of life and political system where people of color—not just Black African, but also South Asian and Jewish citizens—experienced the worst depredations of a totalitarian regime bent on controlling every aspect of daily living.

They, like Dr. G., knew what it was like to live on the fringes of society, what it was like to live as a second-class citizen, existing in constant fear of what the next day would bring with the very real possibility of imprisonment or death at the hands of megalomaniacs bent on total control. So, Dr. G. identified with Chicagoans of color, sympathized with them, and shared a special bond and affinity for them.

However, of all the wisdom Dr. G. imparted to me, out of all the admirable behavior he displayed to my fellow medical students and I, the following episode stands out as the most memorable and thought-provoking.

It was the medical student's duty to present cases during the psychiatric department's morning conferences. That day, I was presenting the rather tragic case of a graduate student in physics who had undergone a psychotic break. It was tragic because this man was brilliant with a mind brimming over with ideas, whose future in the field held much promise until he was laid low by mental illness. This unfortunate young man, who was the same age as I was, could have been a poster child for the adage, "There is a thin line between brilliance and madness." To compound the misfortune even further, I was now going over the details of how this sick young man was beginning to show signs of hebephrenia, which is a more aggressive, impulsive, chaotic, and violent form of schizophrenia.

The professor in charge of the morning conference was a man I'll call "Dr. E." If there was ever a character foil to Dr. G.'s earthy, amiable, humble, honest, outgoing, and self-effacing way of doing medicine, it was Dr. E.

Dr. E. was cold, clinically detached, calculating, and controlled, cultivating all the proper relationships as he climbed the ladder of academic medicine. He was pompous, full of himself, always self-assured, and usually self-absorbed. In contrast to Dr. G.'s decidedly no-necktie-and sneakers-while-doing-patient-care mien, Dr. E. wore suits tailored made for him by Michigan Avenue haberdasheries and a gold Rolex to complete the image of a successful doctor. He drove a Porsche 911, which he conspicuously parked in a prominent parking spot in the hospital garage. In contrast, Dr. G., rode an old ten-speed, dodging Hyde Park traffic to get to work every day, except when it was too windy in the Windy City. On those days, Dr. G. rode the CTA bus.

It was widely known that Dr. G. and Dr. E. did not get along. There was an unspoken animosity between them simmering, yet never quite boiling over.

During my case presentation, Dr. E. asked me to expound further upon my unfortunate patient's more paranoid tendencies as paranoia is often a component of schizophrenia. These delusions were many, and as interpreted through the relatively innocent cultural prism of the early 1990s, quite bizarre. I went down the list:

"The patient believes that the government is reading his mail. He also believes that his phone conversations are being monitored. He believes that other members of the physics department are out to get him. The patient believes that the head of the physics department is having him followed."

As I went through the unfortunate litany of the patient's misguided beliefs, I spied Professor G. entering the auditorium from the rear. Another professor sitting towards the front stood deferentially, offering Dr. G. his seat, but Dr. G. waved him off, preferring as always to hang back and sit in the rear with the interns, residents, and medical students, as he always did. He sat and produced from a brown paper bag a bagel smothered in cream cheese that, no doubt, one of his friends in the cafeteria had made personally for him. He listened thoughtfully, eating his bagel as I recited my patient's persecutory delusions.

I continued, "The patient believes his girlfriend is poisoning him, that the CIA is taking control of the university, that campus security is opening his mail, and that aliens are inserting thoughts into the brain of the university president."

As the paranoid beliefs became more bizarre, some snickering could be heard in the auditorium.

I concluded, "In brief, it seems that the patient believes that everyone is out to get him."

The snickering erupted into some open laughter, which continued for some moments.

Then an eastern European voice interjected, with authority, "Well, maybe somebody is *really* out to get this poor bloke Hey? Hey?"

The room fell silent.

The owner of the voice was, of course, Dr. G.

He continued, "Has anyone considered the possibility that somebody *really* is out to get this young man? The physics department is not known for its collegiality. In fact, it *is* incredibly cutthroat over there, hey? Hey?"

He took another bite from his bagel.

Nervous murmurings were now throughout the auditorium where there was previously laughter.

Dr. E., in an attempt to regain control of the conference, said, "Dr. G.! I see that you've finally decided to grace us with your presence! Did you have something to add?"

Between chews of his bagel, Dr. G. replied, "I was simply making the point that given the realities of the academic environment at this university, of which you are a shining example, Dr. E., that at least some of the beliefs of young Villaruz's unfortunate patient may not be delusional but perhaps all too real, hey?"

"You can't be serious, Dr. G.," Dr. E. said dismissively, with an arrogant smirk on his face.

"I'm deadly serious," Dr. G. replied, with a hint of menace, eyeing Dr. E. warily as he took another bite from his bagel. "And Dr. E, it's disgraceful that you should permit laughter at this young man's very sad case, hey? We're trying to teach professionalism, hey?"

"Come now, Dr. G., be reasonable," Dr. E. said, attempting to defuse the situation and maintain some professional decorum at the conference.

"I assure you, I'm in complete possession of all of my faculties, and I'm being completely reasonable."

"I see. You talk as if you're speaking from your own personal experience, Dr. G."

At that moment, fire flashed in Dr. G.'s normally benign and friendly eyes. He put his bagel down and stood up, saying, "What did you just say, Dr. E.? Hey?"

Dr. E., sensing he had crossed a line, visibly sunk back into his seat, but wanting to save face with the department he was supposed to be a leader in, smiled nervously and repeated himself, "I said it sounds like you're speaking from your own experience, Dr. G."

"My own experience?! My own experience?! My own experience you say, Dr. E.?! Hey! HEY?!" Dr. G. bellowed as he took a few steps, with fists clenched, towards Dr. E., and we all took a deep breath. Everyone was shocked at this show of anger and aggression from always approachable, amiable, and affable old Dr. G.

But then, Dr. G. visibly checked himself. He stopped, closed his eyes, took a deep breath, pondering wordlessly. He was silent for a few moments.

I remember that at that moment, you could hear a pin drop. It seemed that nobody took a breath.

Dr. G. re-opened his eyes. They had a far-off, dreamy look to them, like he was remembering a figment from his past. He reflected for a few moments, composing himself even further. No longer yelling, but almost in a whisper, he said, "My personal experiences, hey Dr. E.? Why yes, I am speaking from my own personal experiences. Because unlike anyone else in this room, beyond anything anyone sitting here can possibly imagine, I know what it's like when someone is *really* out to get you. My personal experience, Dr. E.? You want to know my personal experience? Here it is."

Standing there in the aisle, Dr. Giraffe took off his white lab coat. He then rolled up his left sleeve and held his forearm up for everyone to see.

There on Dr. G.'s forearm, fading but as indelible as any other deformity or scar that acts as a perpetual reminder of a past trauma that could never possibly be forgotten, but looking like a bad tattoo, was the old man's concentration camp number. It had been seared into his young skin so long ago by a Nazi brand, when he was barely out of childhood.

We all gasped. Some of the other Jews—and even some Gentiles—began to weep openly. I had seen these marks in the movies or in documentaries about the war, but I had never seen them for real until that day when Dr. G., *Professor G.,* revealed his branding to us in all his righteous anger.

He continued steadily and with no hint of animosity, with a tone of resignation and forgiveness, "Here is my personal experience, Dr. E.," pointing to the ancient tattoo with his index finger. "This is my personal experience, hey? Because sometimes..." he looked at the residents, interns, and medical students towards the back of the room, "...because sometimes, sometimes, people *really are out to get you.* Hey? Hey?!"

The old man went on, still facing the younger people at the conference, "Perhaps if we had been more 'paranoid' in Germany during the 1930s, or in South Africa in the 1960s, more people would be alive today hey? Hey?! Remember, my young friends, that not everyone has the best, most noble and pure intentions. They're promising a utopia, *lebensraum,* and the good life one moment, but there's always a cost, hey? Hey?! And before you know it, they're breaking glass windows, burning books, and herding people who disagree with them into death camps or segregated townships. Here's the proof, hey? Hey?!" as he motioned once again to the dehumanizing mark on his left arm that decades ago had robbed him of his dignity, reducing him to a mere number, mere property, another piece of meat, just another asset.

Then Dr. G. calmly pointed an accusing finger at Dr. E., saying evenly, "My personal experience is that they did this to my people while elites like him, in their nice clothes, with their fancy watches and expensive cars, stood by and did absolutely nothing, hey? Hey?"

All you could hear in the room was the weeping I had mentioned before.

Dr. G. picked up his lab coat, walked back to his seat, quietly packed up what was left of his bagel, and turned to leave.

Turning a final time to the younger people in the room, Dr. G. implored us now with a few tears in his eyes as well, "My personal experience, my dear young friends, is that the Shoah was real, hey? My personal experience is to beware of those promising you a good and easy life, yet always at the expense of a few unfortunates, hey? If even one innocent life is sacrificed for the sake of your 'better world,' that's a very evil thing, hey? My personal experience is that not everyone you meet has your best interests in mind, hey? And above all, remember this, *Just because you're paranoid doesn't mean people aren't out to get you. Sometimes, people REALLY ARE out to get you.*"

And, with that, while adjusting his kippah, the constant reminder that always above him was a compassionate, merciful, all-seeing, and all-knowing God, Dr. G. left the room in silence.

I'd never before heard a speech as meaningful, as prophetic, as fraught with warning, as Dr. G.'s was on that day. It was perhaps the best lecture I attended during my four years at Pritzker and the best of all the teaching I received as a medical student. The priceless wisdom imparted to me during the G.-E. confrontation, it turns out, had nothing at all to do with medicine.

Dr. G. has since passed on. I remember reading that he was ailing in an alumni newsletter in the early 2000s. A classmate I ran into at a conference not too long ago informed me that Dr. G. passed in 2011. I mourned for him.

However, his example is always in my mind and heart, inspiring me, challenging me. His example continues to guide me not only during my everyday interactions with patients but helps form the prism through which I view current events.

I remember leaving the auditorium that day after witnessing the G.-E. confrontation with the feeling that my perceptions of what was going on in the world around me had changed completely. It was a transformative experience. I realized that my viewpoints would never be the same. I began to look at cultural issues more critically, and from different perspectives, especially from that of the marginalized and powerless. Since that day, I have read and heard of many progressive concepts and ideas in my life and forgotten most of them. However, Dr. G.'s words still ring clear and true across the decades. With the tumultuous events of the last few years, I have been thinking back on much of the wisdom Dr. G. imparted more and more.

He is a shade of my past, an unlikely prophet, reminding me always that those in power do not always have the best of intentions or our best interests in mind, that utopia always comes at the expense of a forgotten, persecuted few. Dr. G.'s life reminds me that it is the promise of the "good life," rainbows and unicorns and coming together one moment, then cancellation, censorship, shaming—or worse—the next. The "worse" part? It could never happen, right? Human civilization has developed beyond that point, right? Sadly, the fading numbers on Dr. G.'s left forearm told us otherwise.

Just because you are paranoid does not mean people are not *really* out to get you. Sometimes, people *really* are out to get you.

And the sad, grand irony of all this?

The most paranoid, then implausible beliefs of that unfortunate physics grad student that I recited so long ago—delusions like the widespread government monitoring of our personal communications, like the intrusion of security agencies and profit-seeking corporations into our personal lives for the sake of security and profit, implausibilities like the insertion of ideas into our heads, not by space aliens, but by the electronic devices and Internet that we are all so enthralled with, paranoid rants of neighbors monitoring and informing on each other lest too large a gathering is held—these ravings of an unfortunate, mentally ill young man, that we so easily discounted back then because it all seemed so outlandish. . .has all come to pass, has it not? In the name of security? In the name of profit?

Maybe we as a society are the ones that need to be a committed to an institution...

Maybe that young man and old man G. were the only sane ones all along...

Maybe...

Just because you're paranoid, doesn't mean people aren't to get you.

Sometimes people *really* are out to get you.

Hey?

❧ 12 ❧

BEST HALLOWEEN TREAT

Written during the rather unusual Halloween of 2020, just before the rather contentious election a few days later. Be not afraid!

Diana and I took Mikhail trick-or-treating last night. It was an idyllic evening for an All Hallows' Eve—brisk weather, crystal-clear skies magnifying the glory of a full harvest moon, with a light breeze gently blowing autumn leaves about our feet as we walked from house to house. It was a relief to see other parents and children out and about doing the same as us on what was a glorious autumn evening. It lent a sense to normalcy to what had been otherwise a highly aberrant year.

In our neighborhood, residents signify their willingness to participate in the festivities by keeping the porch lights on to welcome the costumed children. It is a sign of the times that slightly less than half of the homes in our community had their porch lights on this year.

Very sad.

And many of those homes that had porch lights on had the Halloween treats unceremoniously dumped into a bucket near the door for the children to anonymously partake of—

not wanting to risk the interpersonal interaction that might cause transmission of a glorified cold virus. I thought that this was rather disappointing because what is Halloween for a child without adults complimenting you on how cool your costume is?

As Diana and I took Misha on his rounds, one of the homes that had its porch lights on was my neighbor's—an older woman named Ruth. This surprised me, as I had barely seen Ruth since the lockdown began. Before then, I would see Ruth almost daily on my way to the mailbox, stopping for a quick chat with her while she sat on her porch reading or drinking tea. Ruth, I figured, had been making herself as scarce as possible because she is in a very high-risk group in terms of COVID mortality.

Yet Ruth's porch light burned brightly last night—a welcoming beacon on a chilly autumn evening in a season of fear and ever-shortening days.

As we climbed the steps to Ruth's porch, I noticed that there was not yet another big bowl of candy for us to unceremoniously and anonymously partake of. Instead, I saw that her door was open, and standing there, like a vision of what everybody's silver haired grandmother should look like, was Ruth herself with a broad smile on her face. Behind her in her living room, I spied a cozy, welcoming fire on her hearth.

"Miss Ruth!" I exclaimed. "It's so nice to see you!"

"Doctor Al, it's been forever!" she said in reply, and then reached out to shake my hand.

This gesture took me by surprise, given the social distancing we have all been forced to live with and have had hammered into our collective consciousness in the last few months.

But I took her hand and shook it affectionately.

She looked behind me and saw Diana carrying Misha, who was dressed in a lion costume. She greeted Diana warmly. To Misha she said, "My, aren't you the world's cutest lion! You've grown so much since I last saw you!"

"Well, Miss Ruth, it has been since March since you've seen him."

Then we all laughed.

Ruth then grabbed some Snickers and Twix from a bowl in her foyer and placed a handful into Misha's trick-or-treating pail. She said, "You're so cute, Misha, so you get extra!" then she dumped another handful into it, much to my son's glee.

Diana could not help herself and asked, "Ruth, you're handing out candy in person. . . aren't you scared of getting COVID?"

Ruth smiled for a few moments, and she seemed to be reflecting.

"Dear, I'm ninety-one years old," she replied.

Now I knew Ruth was up there, but not *that* up there and with a very high (30%) mortality rate from COVID should she get the disease. Yet here she was, on Halloween, handing out candy *in person.*

"I'm ninety-one years old," Ruth continued. "Dear, I've lived through the Great Depression. I lost an older brother and an uncle in World War Two. My son was killed in Vietnam. I've outlived two husbands. For the last six months, I've done nothing but sit in this house," she said with frustration, gesturing to the walls that had confined her.

Ruth then said something that I will never forget:

"*I am so tired of being afraid. I am so tired of living in fear,* so I am going to hand out candy on Halloween no matter what my daughter or some doctor on TV tells me to do—no offense intended, Doctor Al."

"None taken, Miss Ruth," I replied, myself irritated by the inconsistency and vacillation surrounding the entire handling of this pandemic.

Then Ruth winked at us. "I'm ninety-one after all. I don't know how many more Halloweens I have in me," she said.

We all laughed again, almost defiantly, against the gloom of the night and impending mortality that awaits us all.

Ruth stroked the top of Misha's head and quietly said to him, "But you have years, *decades* even, don't you Misha?" Her voice trailed off. It seemed that she was remembering the sacred memories of her ninety Halloweens past. Perhaps she was remembering the son she used to take trick-or-treating on beautiful fall evenings like this one, the child she lost in Vietnam. The thought of that broke my heart as I looked at Ruth and my son, realizing that almost a *century* separated these two, yet here they were together on this Halloween night.

I thought to myself, *There is no such thing as coincidence in life, is there? Everything happens for a reason.* Take this unlikely juxtaposition of Ruth and my son, for instance. The very young, and the very old—the two most vulnerable segments of our society brought together for one fleeting, miraculous instance. One generation passing the baton to the other.

Ruth snapped back to the present. She said, "Just remember *this* Diana, Misha, Doctor Al. . . tough times don't last, but tough people do!" This was not the first time I had heard this particular truism from someone in Ruth's generation, but it was affirming and wonderful to hear again just the same.

And with that, we parted. We left Ruth to her sacred memories.

But I will always remember Ruth's resilience, her faith, her single-mindedness. Seeing it last night was the best treat of our Halloween.

Aren't you tired of being so afraid?

Aren't you tired of living in fear?

Ruth is.

❧ 13 ❧

WORSE FATES

Written just before Christmas 2021. With another Christmas of isolation looming, I remembered that faith, hope, and love are the most effective remedies.

I was getting ready for work yesterday when I heard a knock on my door. It was one of neighbors, a woman in her late sixties, whose mother is a resident in one of the local nursing homes. I will call this neighbor Joan. She had a worried expression on her face. She said she wanted to solicit my medical advice. The subsequent conversation went like this:

Joan: "Dr. Al. I hope I'm not bothering you. Do you have a moment to answer a question?"

Me: "Of course, Joan. What is it?"

Joan: "My granddaughter just found out that her college roommate tested positive for COVID."

Me: "OK..."

Joan: "But I had my granddaughter over for a visit yesterday. We kept our social distance, though."

Joan made a gesture with her arms indicating the amount of separation they maintained. I sensed where this line of questioning was headed, so I asked her:

Me: "Does your granddaughter have any symptoms?"

Joan: "Her voice is a little hoarse, and her nose is a little runny."

Me: "So now, you want to know if you can still visit your mom at her nursing home on Christmas, right?"

She had previously told me how excited she was at the prospect of visiting her mother on Christmas Day this year after not being allowed to see her last Christmas, due to COVID.

Joan: "Well, yes, Dr. Al. I want to know what you think I should do."

Me: "Are you vaccinated, Joan?"

Joan: "Yes."

Me: "And your mom is vaccinated, right?"

Joan: "Yes, of course"

Me: "And you have no symptoms, right, Joan?"

Joan: "No, I do not."

Not wishing to mislead my neighbor at that point, my anxiety grew as my physician's mind was filled with some of the non-sensical and often contradictory "facts" surrounding the transmission of COVID. I thought frantically for a few moments then came to a sudden realization. It was like a lightbulb coming on in my head, a real eureka moment.

With absolute clarity and conviction I began, "Joan, I think you should go see your mom. You're a wonderful daughter. You've done what you can and taken the necessary precautions. But to be frank, who knows how much longer your mom will be with us? There are no guarantees in life. This may be her last Christmas. There's no way to know. . ."

My neighbor looked relieved after my declarations, as if I had affirmed her intuition. Yet a part of her remained frightened and uncertain.

She persisted. "But Dr. Al, *are you sure?*"

I replied: "When it comes to this virus, I don't know what to believe. I see, hear, experience, and read so many conflicting things. When it comes to this disease, I'm not sure about anything. But what I am *sure* of, for certain, is that if your mom doesn't see you and your family for a second Christmas in a row, it will *kill* her just as *surely* as COVID could. *That*, I am *sure* of!"

Joan thought on this. Her eyes grew teary. She offered me her hand, and I took it, as Wuhan virus covered as it may be. Her face took on a defiant expression.

"Dr. Al, thank you. And Merry Christmas!"

There are fates far worse than an outcome this glorified virus could possibly conjure up for us. Pandemic or not, we are presented with singular moments in all of eternity in which we are called to give love. These moments pass in an instant, never to repeat themselves—gone forever. And there are powers at work in this world greater and more loving than anything this imminent "winter of death" can possibly bring to bear.

We are not alone and without help.

Merry Christmas.

❧ 14 ❧

PEACE ON EARTH

During the holidays a few years ago, I assumed care of an elderly man who had been ejected from the nursing home in which he had been residing, leading to his transfer to our emergency department (ED). The reason for this rejection was that he was supposedly displaying increasingly aggressive and belligerent behaviors, so he was now considered a threat to nursing home residents and staff.

As a result, he had been unceremoniously foisted off onto our emergency department, so that we could figure out what to do with him. The nursing home did not want him back, and his family did not want to be burdened any further. So, he took up residence in one of our psychiatric rooms until we could find a disposition.

We, meaning the ED nurses, physicians, social workers, and security staff, had become the old man's de facto family. Sadly, this old man's case was not an isolated anomaly. Anybody who would be willing to spend time with us would perhaps be very surprised to see that our emergency departments are the repository of the unwanted flotsam and jetsam of our society—beings of all ages, from the very young to the very old, of all creeds, ethnicities, and socioeconomic strata.

We live in a culture where, sadly, people are increasingly being seen as mere "human infrastructure"—human beings as just another asset or commodity to be bought, sold, or "written off" as unsalvageable, as this unfortunate old man had been. He had become completely disposable, consigned to the care of complete strangers in order to facilitate the ease, lifestyle choices, and convenience of others.

Your kid is acting up and too hard to handle? Call the cops to do an emergency petition and have them brought to the ED! Tired of taking care of your elderly parent? Bring them to the ED under the premise of addressing any one of a number of non-emergent, chronic complaints, *then* abruptly tell us that you can no longer care for them and leave them to linger with us for days. In the meantime, our dutiful but overworked social work staff labor to find a place where they can live out the rest of their days.

For make no mistake, friends. Your emergency departments have become the wastebaskets for an increasingly self-absorbed, self-indulgent, and ultimately self-destructive society to jettison those who are deemed to be an inconvenience.

However, we do not see ourselves as a trash heap. We are more like a safety net. We are a safe harbor in a storm-tossed world. We are the last remaining light when all other lights have been extinguished.

We are not a trash heap.

And people are not trash.

Or infrastructure.

I figured I should go and assess this old man while I had the time, before my shift got too out of hand, as ED shifts tend to do. I noted that the old man with a supposed "history of violence" had already been there for two days.

On my way to his room, I ran into the nurse who was taking care of him and asked her how the old man was doing, if there had been any disruptive outbursts. She replied, "He's been good. Sleeps most of the time. Only speaks up when he's hungry or needs to use the bathroom. He's been a good patient. Very polite. Hasn't been violent or anything. Have no idea why the nursing home sent him here."

The nurse then rolled her eyes and shrugged off-handedly. I asked her, "Has he gotten any sedation?"

She shook her head, saying a quick "Nope."

It was all very underwhelming as far as emergency department instances of violence and disruption go.

When I walked into the old man's room, he was sleeping soundly, covered in a blanket with his back turned to me—not surprising as it was only slightly past six in the morning. I didn't turn the room light on, not wanting to provoke an undesirable response.

As I did a quick assessment, listening gingerly to his heart and lungs so as not to wake him, I noticed that he was clutching an object to his chest. I was surprised by this observation, as all patients unfortunate enough to become guests in any of our bare bones psychiatric rooms are supposed to have all personal items confiscated from them for their own safety, of course. My curiosity and instinct for self-preservation piqued. I gently pulled back the old man's covers in order to see what he was embracing so tightly.

It was a baby doll. Little baby hands, little baby feet. It had a permanent, contented, perfectly peaceful smile painted on its face. The doll was dressed in pajamas adorned with smiling teddy bears, friendly rabbits, rainbows, and puffy clouds—everything associated with a joyful but fleeting childhood.

It was the kind of toy you could probably pick up at the Dollar Store for a pittance.

Yet the sleeping old man held it to his heart it with a ferocity and firmness, indicating that it was what he cherished most deeply. He was protecting and sheltering—indeed, *loving*—this proxy child with every ounce of his being. Though he slumbered on, every indication was the old man loved this cheap toy as if it were a real child. He would give his life for this child, give anything for this child, for his vise-like embrace made it look like he was holding onto this proxy child for dear life.

It was probably his only remaining real possession, lonely and abandoned as he was, and it clearly meant everything to him. Yes, the old man was holding onto the baby for dear life, as if he was sure that this child would somehow save him in the end.

He clearly adored his toy, this trinket. And though it be only made of cheap plastic, it was nonetheless the child of his heart.

"Papa!" the child's painted and perpetually smiling face seemed to be saying to him.

"Papa! Papa! I love you! Thank you for taking care of me!"

And the ferocity of the old man's embrace seemed to say, "I love you, my child. Now *save me* too!"

"*Save me*, my child!"

Well, truth be told, the pathos of this entire scene stopped me in my tracks. I've been doing this emergency medicine gig for twenty years now, and very few events still give me pause and make me stop to think. All of the little daily traumas I experience whenever I go to work are now like so much water off of a duck's back after two decades of this stuff.

But this sight literally stopped me in my tracks.

I was deeply moved by what I was beholding.

I was overwhelmed by a hard-to-verbalize combination of childhood memories of my own dad, loneliness, regret over my own callous insensitivities, poignancy, sadness, and sentimentality over what I was beholding.

I had to choke back tears. . .and anger.

It was not just a little anger at the realization that here we are, the most affluent and technologically savvy nation on earth, a place where we wield the god-like power of obtaining our hearts' desires with a few finger sweeps on our cellphones, a country where we enjoy the highest standard of living in the world, and all we can offer a lonely old man at the end of his days is a cheap dollar store toy to give him comfort as he is consigned to the oblivion of a nightmarish facility for troubled elderly in some big city where no one really knows him. We smugly impress ourselves by possessing the cutting edge in everything from cell phones to vaccines, but we have yet to find any remedy for basic human loneliness and wretchedness.

The entire spectacle was pathetic.

But there was a peacefulness about the whole pathetic scene too.

For here, in this darkened and quiet room, within a remote nook of our loud and chaotic emergency department reserved for the mentally ill was a vision of complete peace—father holding child as both rested peacefully. The parent was caring for the child, sheltering the child, protecting the child— exactly as life is meant to be. It was an island of absolute tranquility in a sea of hustle and bustle, a cacophony of alarms and human tragedies that transpire within a daily basis in our

ED. To behold such a vision of peace, however fleeting, in the midst of so much chaos, felt like a privilege.

Indeed, it was a blessing.

In the midst of chaos—peace!

That is one of the greatest desires of the human heart.

I gently replaced the covers over the old man and the child of his heart, grateful that I did not wake him and interrupt whatever modicum of solace he was experiencing in so simple a pleasure—the joy of holding his child in unmolested tranquility. I exited the room as quietly as possible, feeling strangely refreshed and renewed, ready to face the remainder of my shift.

I had to compose myself before taking leave of the old man and his child-doll.

As I walked back into the main ED, I ran into our security guard, a beefy, ominous appearing, but in reality, very good-natured, soft-spoken, and deeply respectful African American man. As I saw him, I winked and smiled saying, "Hey Tyrone, I thought security was supposed to confiscate all personal items from psych patients?!"

The security guard smiled back and said conspiratorially, "Come on now, Doc. Let's keep it between us, okay? That old man has nothing left. I figured what's the harm in letting him keep the toy? It keeps him calm. Ain't no harm in it, Doc. It's not like he's gonna assault anyone with a toy doll, right?"

"I feel you, my friend. I feel you. Our secret, okay?" I replied.

Our vow of secrecy sealed, the security guard and I did a fist bump, our pact cemented, our conspiracy secure from the depredations of thoughtless conformists and stifling rule followers.

It turns out much may depend on the little mercies of anonymous security guards, I thought. Portentous events may indeed hinge on the actions of seemingly insignificant yet noble people who know in their hearts that mercy is at the heart of any truly just law or rule.

Who would have thought?

Yes, the image of the old man and his child doll has never wandered far from my consciousness ever since.

It comes to me as I hold my own boys, Misha and Sasha, reading to them, then rocking them to sleep. I think of it as I feel their bodies, spun from star dust out of the inconceivable vastness of the universe, grow heavy with slumber as I hold them. Holding my boys, knowing great inner happiness and peace in these singular moments in all of eternity, I inhabit a small, defiant island of solace in a time filled with chaos, uncertainty, and upheaval—an almost unhinged, constant state of flux that has grown even more frighteningly accelerated in the last two years.

My time with my boys is one of my only remaining sanctuaries in a decidedly unsettled, pestilential time where the ebb and flow of normal daily living, which we once took for a given, can no longer be taken for granted. My time with my boys gives me peace in the midst of all the chaos and the audacity to hope despite the darkness which threatens to devour everything.

As I hold my slumbering boys during this holy season, I think of holiness itself. Now, I am far from a perfect person, much less a perfect Christian. But really, what does it mean to be holy? What does holiness entail? As I hold, care for, and protect my boys, I have come to the realization that what I was doing was holy. It was holy because it was exactly what God meant for a father to do—to hold, care, and provide for, and ultimately protect his children.

I realized that holiness is not only to be found in dramatic, grand acts of heroism, martyrdom, sainthood, and self-sacrifice. I concluded that we are holy every time we are as God wishes us to be, even if it is doing something as hidden, quiet, and seemingly insignificant as being good parents caring for our children.

Holiness is comprised, simply enough, in being exactly as God wishes you to be each and every moment of your life—as a parent, as a professional, as a child to your own parents, as a sibling, as a friend, as a citizen, as a co-worker, or even as a good-natured security guard who puts kindness and mercy over the letter of the law. Holiness is being the best you can be wherever you happen to be in life and for those God puts in your path.

And it gives God pleasure.

Holding Misha and Sasha in my arms, I think of the old man sleeping in the psych room, fiercely clutching a cheap doll, holding on for dear life, his heart crying out, "*Save me!*" I realize that alone and abandoned at the end of all things, the old man was desperately trying to recreate a sacred moment of consolation and solace with a long-lost child, present only in his sacred memories.

I understand that the old man was trying to experience once again the quiet joy, comfort, and peace I was feeling now, holding my living and breathing children in my own arms. I understand now, that in the midst of all the dislocation and rejection he was undergoing, and in the midst of all the chaos, the old man was struggling to recreate a memory of a time when he had known complete *holiness* and *happiness*—a happier time when he was holy and pleasing to God, for he was being exactly what he was meant to be.

"Papa, Papa!" the child cried out.

In return, with a humble holiness, the old man's heart reassured the child, "I am here, my child, do not be afraid!" while clutching his beloved more tightly to his bosom, as only a parent can. His lonely and sorrowful soul then implored the child he clutched so fiercely in his arms, "Now *save me*, my child!"

But can a Child really save us? Save anyone?

If you are a believer, Christmas is an opportunity to commemorate, celebrate, and honor the fact that yes, a Child did come into our midst to do just that very thing. . .to save us.

This Child was born to first time migrant pauper parents, far from home, in a time of chaos and upheaval. . .a helpless one born to parents who themselves were powerless against the dictates of a far-off authority who decreed that they be counted, like livestock, like any other asset to be bartered, bought, and sold, like human infrastructure. He was a child of royal lineage, but nonetheless a member of a captive and conquered race, administered by the most ruthless and brutally efficient military the ancient world had ever seen. . .a child born in a filthy manger that smelled of dung and urine to exhausted, unwashed, and frightened parents.

Much chaos. Yes. And great upheaval.

But this chaos was redeemed by the holiness of simple and lowly people, hidden and seemingly insignificant in the grand scheme of things but great in the eyes of God because they were exactly as He wished them to be.

This chaos was redeemed by the unexpected kindness of the innkeeper's wife, who took pity on a forlorn young couple and directed them to a disused, yet warm and sturdy shelter.

This hopeless time was redeemed by shepherds who lived lives of isolation and want in the fields yet knew a true miracle when they saw it—shepherds who came to stand vigil not over a flock of sheep, but this time to keep watch over a young family because they knew in their hearts it was a good and noble task to undertake. This chaos was redeemed by oxen and sheep that shared the manger with the Child, His first playmates, their animal warmth keeping the cold at bay.

The chaos, the upheaval, the dislocation, the fear, and the filth, all redeemed by the holiness of good and humble beings who knew that mercy was at the heart of the law.

And in the midst of all of that ancient chaos—behold, *peace*—a singular, defiant moment of peace, redemption, and solace in the face of calamitous and momentous events which threaten to sweep all of us up in their irresistible torrent. This was an unlikely instance of heaven meeting earth in such an unlikely way in such an unexpected place.

However, real life is like that, right? Real life is bills, sick kids, dirty laundry, lack of staff, and absent leadership at work, with way too much to do. Real life is complex. Real life is difficult. Real life is decidedly not idyllic—it's. . .well. . .*real*. Real life can be a big mess. Real life is filled with difficult moments. Yet these moments, as trying as they are, can be redeemed by holiness by returning to the simplicity of being exactly as God wants us to be.

By holiness, in being exactly what a loving and merciful God wishes us to be at each at every moment in our lives, we can create sublime moments of peace, joy, and beauty in the midst of all the chaos. In any situation, we can redeem all the difficulties, disappointments, pain, and hardship with holiness by regaining the simplicity of being just what God calls us to be.

Peace can therefore be experienced in the most unexpected of moments, during the most chaotic of times, in the most unlikely of places.

Even in the guise of a lonely, abandoned old man reliving the holiness of his long-lost fatherhood by holding onto a toy doll for dear life. This was a moment of peace made possible by a security guard practicing holiness in his own way, being exactly what God meant him to be—kind, merciful, patient, and understanding.

This Christmas, I am trying to remember that holiness is not abstract, complex, or unattainable. I am trying to remember that holiness is, instead, *simplicity*. Holiness is being simple—it is being exactly what we were meant to be.

And with the simplicity of a child, I do believe that a Child has come to save us.

I believe that a Child *can* save us, for my own Misha and Sasha have saved me.

A Child can save us.